CW00329321

# The Secrets of Communication

# Secrets of Communication

## Be Heard and Get Results

# PETER THOMSON

SIMON & SCHUSTER

LONDON · SYDNEY · NEW YORK · TOKYO · SINGAPORE · TORONTO

First published in Great Britain by Simon & Schuster Ltd, 1996
A Viacom Company

Copyright © Peter Thomson, 1996

This book is copyright under the Berne Convention.
No reproduction without permission.
All rights reserved.

The right of Peter Thomson to be identified as author
of this work has been asserted by him in accordance
with the Copyright, Designs and Patents Act, 1988.

**Simon & Schuster Ltd**
**West Garden Place**
**Kendal Street**
**London**
**W2 2AQ**

**Simon & Schuster of Australia Pty Ltd**
**Sydney**

A CIP catalogue record for this book is
available from the British Library

ISBN 0-684-81665-2

Typeset in Goudy Old Style
by Hewer Text Composition Services, Edinburgh
Printed and bound in Great Britain
by Clays Ltd, St Ives plc

# Acknowledgements

M any people have helped me with the production of this book. I am delighted to have the opportunity to thank them all and in particular:

my four sons James, Richard, Stephen and David for being the testing ground to prove so many of the ideas;

my good friend David Hughes for his faith in me and constant support;

to all my friends for being the willing victims of my methods and techniques;

and to my wife Sharon for her constant support and positive attitude and for her help in organising our lives to enable me to have the time to produce this book.

# Contents

# Foreword

Of all the creatures on the face of the earth it is only the strange two-legged one who walks in an upright manner who has managed to gain dominion over all the rest . . .

. . . MANKIND!

And yet . . . we aren't the largest,
　　　　　　　we aren't the strongest
　　　　　　　　　　　we aren't the most brightly coloured!

We can't swim underwater without the aid of an artificial air supply, we can't fly in the air without the aid of some device to keep us airborne and without the aid of clothing of some description we would be unable to survive in many regions of the world. Yet despite all these apparent handicaps we have become the dominant species on earth.

　　Why? . . . simply because we can communicate with our own kind in such a manner as to be able to share the most complex of ideas, theories and messages.

　　Just think if fish or elephants or eagles could have communicated their ideas in the way in which humans are able to speak . . . what a different world we would live in today.

## Welcome to *The Secrets of Communication*

The purpose of this book is to enable me to share with you numerous ideas, methods and techniques that – regardless of your social position, regardless of your field of commercial operation and regardless of age, sex, colour, creed or financial standing – will enable you to use more of that remarkable skill we all possess: **The Secrets of Communication**.

The ability to converse is one of our greatest, if not our greatest asset. Constant learning and practice in this area is essential for us all. For, if we are able to communicate our ideas, our thoughts and our commercial and social messages more clearly and more completely to whoever is prepared to listen, then we are certain to be more successful – more successful in any endeavour.

There are so many benefits for us in every area of our lives if we understand the process of conversation, the power of language and the skills of persuasion.

When I look back over the activities of my life I realise that every success and every failure can be attributed directly to my ability to communicate, my ability to understand what was really happening in every written and spoken exchange.

In a business environment I have been fortunate to have achieved what some might call success and I attribute this to my early understanding that *people* are what make the difference to one's life. It seemed to me that to be commercially successful I needed to have people help me in that endeavour. In some way I would have to influence those people to share my vision of the future and see sufficient benefit for themselves in ensuring that our objectives were reached, our goals achieved and our targets hit or surpassed.

How could I do this without being manipulative, without resorting to the often used management techniques of the carrot and the stick, without creating resentment of any sort in those people?

**Only by persuasion. Persuasion by conversation.**

How will you benefit from the information contained within these pages?

- You will have better conversations.
- You will be more persuasive.
- You will have enhanced relationships with everyone with whom you interact in both business and social conversations.
- You will be able to handle difficult communication situations with ease.
- You will have more success (whatever your personal definition of that emotive word).
- You will have a great deal of fun listening to others and watching their body language.

As we go through the hundreds of ideas in *The Secrets of Communication* I will share with you a variety of methods and techniques that will enable you to utilise these thoughts to obtain maximum benefit.

There will be numerous examples of the ideas in action.

It will be necessary for you to customise the ideas to your own activities, to your own style, to you!

A thought that is relevant to all the ideas, methods and techniques that we shall explore throughout this book is that we are all in the persuasion business, regardless of our job description, our job title or even our job function.

Throughout each day we are persuading. We could use such words as negotiating, marketing, selling, influencing, telling, promoting, encouraging, stimulating, inspiring, advertising, vending, trading, or even delegating, leading or managing. But all these skills involve the powers of persuasion, so that is the word used throughout the book. We persuade others to accept our ideas, our products, our services, our concepts or simply ourselves.

Sometimes that persuasion is on ourselves. The self talk, the self dialogue in which we all indulge every single day. From the moment we open our eyes to the moment we close them again at the end of the day. 'Shall I get up now or have just a few more minutes in bed?', 'Shall I wear that red blouse today?', 'What shall I have for breakfast, lunch or dinner?'

All conversation, all persuasion.

Imagine a situation at work. You want to ask a member of your team to undertake a certain task. If you TELL him or her in a dictatorial tone, and with the gestures of body language which say 'I'm in charge', without regard for that person's feelings, then yes, you will get the job done. However with persuasion in your voice and body, the task will still be done but this time with a glad heart. Often this produces a much better result. A good result for the other person and you. A true win/ win situation.

Peter Thomson

# 1    The Power of Active Listening

Our first area of examination is that fascinating one of Active Listening. Although it is the reverse side of the coin of conversation skills it is nevertheless an extremely important area.

Let's have some fun together as I share with you ten active listening questions. You will find the answers on page 217.

## Active Listening Test

1   Divide 40 by a half and add 15. What is the answer?
2   In Scotland is a man allowed by law to marry his widow's sister?
3   Which is the correct English?
    Nine and five **is** thirteen or nine and five **are** thirteen?
4   How many **cubic yards** of dirt are there in a hole which measures 6 yards long, 3 yards wide and 1 yard deep?
5   When an ocean-going liner is repainted it receives 25 coats of paint.
    Which coat goes on the first?
6   A train leaves Birmingham at 7.00 a.m. for the 100-mile journey to London; it travels at 100 m.p.h. Also at 7.00 a.m. a train leaves London for the 100-mile journey to Birmingham; it travels at 50 m.p.h. Which train will be closer to London when they meet, the train that left Birmingham or the train that left London?

7   Which of these three would see most clearly in total darkness:
     a leopard, an owl or a bat?

8   You have two coins which total 30p. Since one of those coins
     is not a 10p. piece, what are the two coins?

9   How many animals of each **species** did Moses take into the
     ark?

10  Before Mount Everest was discovered, what was the highest
     mountain on earth?

Well, I wonder how well you did with that test? In years of using
it at various in-house and open seminars, I have found that out
of ten questions the average score has been just four!

If you were to take another test straightaway, I am certain
that you would have a different feeling regarding your listening
skills. Your antennae would be out, your ears would be pricked
up. You would be listening *actively*.

I like to think of listening in this way. Imagine that you are
watching a wildlife TV documentary and the programme is about
big felines, perhaps lions. The picture shows a lion lying absolutely
still, no movement whatsoever. Now it may be that the lion is
asleep or perhaps it is just waiting to pounce. We would feel the
difference, wouldn't we? Well, that is how we should be listening.
Not quite waiting to pounce on the speaker, but listening *actively*.

## The Six Levels of Listening

### 1. The Glazed Eyes

I am certain that everyone has had the experience of being
turned off from the speaker and staring into the middle distance.
We are caught up in our own thoughts and, although hearing
the sound of the spoken word, we are not really listening at all.

### 2. Automatic Response

This is the classic situation of one partner coming home after a
busy day at the office to the other partner who has been at

home all day. One partner has had enough of talking, the other partner is dying to talk.

'Have you had a good day at the office?' Automatic 'Yes'.

'Did you get that order?' Automatic 'Yes'.

'Do you want fish for dinner?' Automatic 'Yes.'

'Is it OK if we stay in tonight?' Automatic 'Yes.'

'Is it OK if I draw all the money out of our savings account and spend it on a new suit?' Automatic 'Yes', followed by the double take, 'What did you say?'

This is a level of listening we sometimes use and know that we shouldn't. It can get us into a great deal of trouble.

### 3. Repeat Last Few Words

This is a level of listening generally called 'listening with one ear', while the other ear is tuned in to our self talk, our internal dialogue. A speaker turns to us and asks (although perhaps more subtly phrased) 'What did I just say?' We are able to retrieve from our marvellous memories just the last few words, in the hope of placating the questioner. Can you remember using this at school, when a teacher didn't bother with any subtlety and bluntly asked 'Thomson, are you listening?' 'Yes,' came the invariable response. 'What did I just say then?' With luck the tape recorder in our minds was able to rewind quickly and play back enough of the last few words to prevent us from getting into trouble.

### 4. Can Answer Questions

At this level real listening begins. If we are able to answer questions about what has been said then we must not only have been listening to what was said but also have thoughts about the information we were hearing. If you are in a role in business or social activities in which it is necessary to ensure that people have clearly understood what you have said, then asking them questions about the content is the ideal way of checking their understanding.

Naturally, unless you are in a dictator role, you would not use the 'What did I just say then?' style of question. You could use some of the following examples:

- 'Bill, so that I am certain that I have explained myself clearly, would you tell me how you see this new computer affecting your job?'
- 'Sally, what do you think will be the impact of these ideas on your team?'
- 'Fred, what's your understanding of that situation?'

These questions are not designed to catch people out. They are simply to check that they have heard what has been said and have taken it in.

## 5. Can Tell Someone Else

This is slightly different from the 'Can answer questions' level insofar as the original speaker will not be present to assist when the listener is explaining the information to a third party. If a listener is confident that they can tell someone else the information then they must have been listening sufficiently actively and attentively to be able to repeat what has been said.

Questions you could use to check this stage would be along the lines:

- 'Tom, would you be able to tell John and Mary about this?'
- 'Jim needs to know this information. Would you be able to tell him, Tom?'
- 'Could you tell your brother about the travel arrangements, Tom?'

Watching Tom's body language and listening to his answer to your question will tell you whether or not Tom has taken in enough of the information to the degree that he can repeat it. Later in the book we will examine a number of body language gestures and ideas that will help you with this level of listening.

### 6. Teach Someone Else

This is the level where someone has not only taken in the information you have given them, not only had thoughts about that information but have been listening so attentively that they could teach that information to someone else, without *you* being present. In other words they could answer questions from someone other than you about the information you have given them.

When we are receiving information, if we can think of ourselves not as the pupil but as the teacher, we will listen actively. For example in your reading of the information in this book think of yourself as a teacher doing research to enable you to teach this information to someone else.

Lee Iacocca, Chief Executive Officer of Chrysler, is reported as saying that, 'The difference between a great company and a mediocre one is its ability to listen to its customers.'

Why is it that people do not always listen actively? More importantly, what can we do about that situation when it occurs?

## Why People Do Not Listen

### Interest Level

It may be that the listener finds the subject-matter boring. They have no interest in the conversation and simply switch off.

### Distractions

The listener could equally be distracted by any number of outside sources, ranging from someone walking by to the telephone ringing or the temperature of the environment. At home it may be the television. I am sure that all parents have had the experience of their children being so intent on their favourite programme that they simply do not hear Mom or

Dad asking what they want for tea, let alone whether they have done their homework. During a car journey the distraction might be the radio or traffic noise or that police car with its siren blaring.

## Self Talk

Perhaps one of the most common reasons for not listening is self talk or what is often called self dialogue. You know this feeling, I'm sure. You are listening to someone who is speaking at about 200 words per minute. Your mind can easily cope with much quicker speech than that, so you start thinking about other things. 'Did I turn off the gas before I left for work?' 'Where shall I go on holiday this year?' 'What shall I do this evening?' So much self talk, so much self dialogue that while hearing the speaker we do not register the incoming information as we might.

## Delivery

Our quality of listening is strongly affected by the delivery of the message, whether through the use of inappropriate language – perhaps too complex, too earthy, too simple – or through the speed of speech – perhaps too s l o w l y   f o r   o u r   m i n d s   or perhaps too quickly.

Maybe the speaker is speaking in a monotone and our minds just fall asleep. And, a common fault among speakers, too much talk without any interaction with the listeners. Have you ever been on the receiving end of that type of speech?

## Body Language

Another major problem may be mismatched body language. The speaker says one thing and his body language says something altogether different. The facial expression is inconsistent with the words, the movements are all out of place. The speaker seems to be uncomfortable or perhaps even lying.

## Eye Contact

Poor eye contact by the speaker may be a problem. We will discuss eye movements in Chapter 4 of this book.

## Waiting to Speak

Could it be that someone has stopped listening because they are simply waiting to speak? I'm certain that you have been in this situation. You are out one evening with friends, perhaps out for dinner or out for a drink and one of your party tells a joke. What often happens is that the joke sparks off another joke in your mind and while the speaker is finishing his or her story you are only just listening, in reality you are *awaiting your turn to speak*. Isn't that true? That is why on the following morning we cannot remember the excellent jokes we heard the night before.

In a business situation we often have similar conversations with similar people and almost know where the conversation will lead. We know what the other person will say in response to our often asked questions. You can be just *waiting to speak* before they have finished speaking.

## Habit Pattern

Some have a habit pattern of not listening. Perhaps they grew up with parents who never listened. Perhaps they have heard before – or think that they have heard before – what you have to say.

## Defence

Finally, lack of listening may be a defence mechanism created to block out the message. Someone in a management role may occasionally have to criticise a member of staff. That member of staff may not like the criticism and simply not listen in order to block out the unpleasant message.

## What to Do!

Well, it's all very well knowing why people do not listen. What can we do when the problem occurs? That is exactly what we are going to cover together in the course of this book. We shall explore how to have better conversations in any situation, how to influence and persuade others to our point of view, how to persuade others to LISTEN to what we have to say.

If we can create in ourselves the habit of active listening then we will receive enormous benefits. We will become more liked. Most people prefer to talk than to listen and need to find a good listener. If we listen actively we will remember more of what's being said. In a moment I will tell you about a technique called the R. R. Method which will enable you to increase your concentration while listening and remember more of what has been said. Active listening and questioning skills are the easiest way to persuade someone else to our point of view and the easiest way to influence others' thoughts and actions.

By actively listening we encourage others to keep on talking. In these days of high-speed communication, when it is said that information is power, encouraging others to keep talking means that they are *giving* more information. If we believe that information is power, then listening means we receive more power.

With active listening we can pay someone else a major compliment by simply saying . . . nothing at all . . . just by giving them our full attention. And of course it is the easiest way to remember good jokes. There are so many benefits. I found that it was the good listeners who received the promotions, not the good talkers. It seems to make good sense to listen.

## When Do We Need to Listen

1   When we need the information that the other party is providing.

This may be in any persuasion role when we have asked a good open-ended question and the other person is responding with a great deal of useful information. Information that will enable us to structure our presentation to meet their needs and desires.

2   We need to listen actively when the person who is talking is important to us. That might be our boss, team leader or manager. It might be a husband, wife, partner or child. In business, our supervisors who give out information will not be impressed if they have to repeat everything they say simply because we do not bother to listen actively.

3   We need to listen particularly attentively whenever there is a possibility of misunderstanding. This might be when the subject being discussed is complex or new to us. It may be when the speaker has an unfamiliar accent. These are occasions when we need to LISTEN!

4   Special care must be taken when the speaker, whether consciously or not, introduces an emotional quality to his or her voice. Those emotions could be anger, frustration, happiness or sadness. It is easy to miss the content because we are affected by the emotional charge of the message. Is that anger directed at us, someone else or simply the speaker's mood?

So, to summarise, we need to listen actively when there is high emotion or the possibility of misunderstanding, when the person is important to us, or when we need the information.

I remember some years ago when I ran a company in Birmingham in England. We were involved in the leasing business. In effect we bought and sold money. Now, as with any product, if you can buy at a better price and still sell at your normal retail price, greater profits can be made. The same principle applies to money. One day I had a meeting with the managing director of a company which was one of our sources of funds in order to persuade him to sell us money at a cheaper rate. I made my proposal and his immediate response was, 'Peter, I don't think that we can do that.' I sat there looking thoughtful for only a few seconds. He continued, 'Well, perhaps there is a way.' I then asked one further open-ended question: 'How would it work?' He went on to tell me his thoughts about an over-ride commission system that would enable him to obtain more business from us and for us to obtain a better rate. That system made my company £12,000 per month, £150,000 per annum and, when the company was sold for a multiplication of profits, a staggering £900,000 for the shareholders. All for a few seconds of active listening. Actively listening to silence.

The rule seems to be: the better we listen and respond to others, the better they will listen and respond to us. The more attention we pay when someone else is talking, the more attention they will pay when we are talking.

## The Steps of Active Listening

### 1. The Right Ratio

Let us think of listening in this way. We have two ears and one mouth; let us use them in that ratio. You probably know what a chess clock is. Such clocks have two faces to enable the players to record the amount of time taken on each move. If we were to use that chess clock to record how long we speak in a conversation as opposed to how long we allow the other person, I am sure that we would give others more time to speak.

If you are involved in business telephone calls, perhaps you could tape-record those calls and then go back through them with a stop watch or chess clock, noting the amount of time each person spoke. Wouldn't that be illuminating?

### 2. Maintain Eye Contact

It is always worthwhile maintaining eye contact while we are listening. It shows others that we are paying attention. I am sure you have heard a parent say to a child: 'Will you LOOK at me when I am talking to you!' That is because we like to see other people's eyes in order to gauge the reaction our words are having. This does not mean that we stare at people. Simply that we maintain regular eye contact.

### 3. Make Notes

The faculty of memory is one of our most remarkable characteristics, even if we don't always have the recall we want, when we want it. Making notes can be an excellent *aide-mémoire*. In some situations it is advisable to ask permission before taking notes. This is seldom refused. If you wish to take a tape recording, it is vital to ask permission.

### 4. Avoid Finishing Other People's Sentences

When we are enthusiastic about the ideas being discussed or if we just can't wait to say our next words, we can easily get into the habit of finishing other people's sentences. They find it extremely frustrating and sometimes we get it wrong!

### 5. Avoid Jumping to Conclusions

You will know this situation. You have similar conversations with similar people during the course of the day. It is easy to get into the habit of jumping to conclusions as to where the sentence is going. Again we can get it wrong. Let's avoid doing it!

### 6. Respond!

A major part of active listening is to let the other party know we are listening. We do this by responding to what they say. This may simply be an odd 'Yes' or 'I see' or even a nod of the head. Have you ever been on the telephone and had to ask the other person: 'Are you still there?' Isn't it an awkward moment? Perhaps both parties are at fault. You for not engaging the other person and the other party for failing to respond.

We also need to respond with our body language.

### 7. Avoid Judging

We all have different ways of speaking – different accents, different catch phrases, different speeds of speech. It is easy to get caught up in listening to those aspects and to miss the content.

One of the criticisms of the jury system is that members of the jury are occasionally believed to decide on innocence or guilt within a few seconds of seeing the defendant, listening only to those parts of the evidence presented to confirm that their first intuition was correct. We can appreciate how that happens. We all like to think that we are expert at instant judgements and no doubt experience has shown us that we do make mistakes in this area.

Regardless of our background, culture or country of origin we all have stereotypes for certain races. The English are often taken to be unemotional, characterised by a stiff upper lip; some people believe that the Irish are slow witted, that the Scots are mean and that the Welsh are xenophobic. A friend of mine on holiday in Italy in conversation with an Italian lady was astonished when the Italian lady said 'I do not know why all you English people send your children away to boarding school!' Obviously this prejudging was taking place on a massive scale.

American stereotypes include 'cheeseheads' from Wisconsin, 'curt' Easterners, 'moralistic and friendly' Mid-Westerners, 'laid back' Californians and so on.

Let's hold back from such judgements wherever possible and really listen to the messages that are being given to us.

## 8. Ask Questions

In later chapters we are going to cover a vast variety of ideas about asking questions. For the moment I mean *ask questions when you do not understand*. We have all been guilty of saying 'Yes, I understand' when nothing could have been further from the truth. We always get caught out later, don't we? Let us have the good sense to say when we do not understand what someone else is saying. I have always found that this pays dividends.

## 9. Ask Core Questions

Often in conversations we fire off a variety of questions just touching the surface of a number of topics or areas. It can be better to ask more questions about one topic than a number of questions about lots of topics. For example, in a business conversation you might ask someone: 'How many branches does your company have?' Their response: 'Ten.' Instead of following with 'How many people does your company employ?' it may be better to ask 'Why do you have ten branches?' The answer to that question may be extremely revealing regarding the company and its future plans.

Continuing to ask 'Why' questions down the same line of questioning can be so useful in obtaining information and used in a self-questioning mode can pull answers from our own minds that would otherwise have lain dormant.

## 10. Pause before Replying

If you have ever been to the theatre you will recognise that the difference between great actors and the not so great has little to do with the script. They all work from the same script, the same words. The difference is HOW the words are said, the inflections and the gaps between the words. Those gaps, those dramatic pauses, are what can bring the play to life.

If you take a small breath before answering another person's questions, rather than jumping in immediately with your answer, it will add power to what you say. It shows that you are giving a considered response, that you thought about it, that it is not just some line you trot out every time this question comes up.

I spend a great deal of my time giving seminars, in-house and open seminars. A man who had been on a personal development and communication skills seminar I had run for his company reported the following to me.

He had been in a meeting with a major client discussing the client's acquisition of a computer system costing £200,000. Having quoted the price to the Financial Director of the client company the man was told: 'We will need at least 10% off that price.' He simply sat there and said nothing. Within a few seconds the Financial Director had changed his tune when he continued, 'Well, at least 5% anyway.'

Very often if you wait before responding, people will continue to talk, giving further information that you may need or be interested to hear.

It is said that the art of conversation is to be interested, not interesting. That's active listening.

## The R. R. Method

A technique of mine for improving listening skills and concentration is the Rapid Repeat Method, and it works like this: Our minds and brains are capable of dealing with vast quantities of data. Some people are able to speak at over 500 words per minute – in which case it is difficult for a listener to absorb all the information. Small wonder then that when someone else is speaking we sometimes indulge in self talk or self dialogue. This can be prevented by using the Rapid Repeat Method. When you are listening to someone, simply repeat what is being said a fraction of a second later, in your mind. Yes, it is that simple. Simply repeat what someone says in your own mind as soon as possible. In other words, rapidly repeat what you have heard. What this does is hold your concentration because in the process you prevent your mind from slipping into self talk. Another benefit is that you will remember far more of the information that the other person presented.

We have all been in social situations, where we have met a number of new people. It is often difficult to remember their names, let alone what they said. By using the R. R. Method you will not only remember their names but you will also recall most, if not all, of the conversation you had with each person.

Use the same tones, the same inflection, the same speed and pitch as the other person. You will find that, while not wishing to jump to conclusions, you will almost become clairvoyant as to the words and direction of the conversation.

If you have not used this idea before I urge you to try it. It is one of the simplest yet most effective methods of active listening.

A word of warning, when you first start to use the Rapid Repeat Method you may find yourself staring at the other person with a vacant look on your face. Take care to animate your face while using the method or you will have others wondering what has happened to you!

So there we have it. Active listening, one of the key skills for success.

One of the simplest ways for you to improve your listening skills using the methods and ideas outlined in this chapter is to make for yourself a key word list of the ideas or steps and then check that list regularly. It is only by practice that our skills improve. Keep the list somewhere that is in constant use – in your diary or day planner – and consult it often. By reminding yourself of these ideas you will see your skills improve to the point that, without thought, you will listen actively to everything that happens around you and be able to remember it.

It is often said that there are none so blind as those who cannot see. We might adapt this to say that there are none so deaf as those who do not listen.

Before we finish this chapter let me share some ideas as to how you can remember what you have read so far and what is contained in the whole of the book.

We remember about 5% of what we hear, 25% of what we see and about 90% or more of what we do. It is well known that if you learned to ride a bicycle as a child you will always be able to do so, even if you have not ridden one for some years. This is simply because we tend to have great memories for actions we have taken the time to perfect. That same skill applies to our ability to communicate.

Take each idea and put it into practice as soon as possible after learning it. That way you will make it your own and have it at your disposal for ever.

Most golfers have a favourite club, one with which they have practised far more than any other. When that club is needed for a particular stroke in a game, the act of taking it from their golf bag will be like shaking hands with an old friend. That is the same with any skill.

While necessity is said to be the mother of invention, repetition is most certainly the master of skill.

# 2    The Subconscious Encoding Process

Our next area of discussion is a fascinating subject. It concerns what happens in someone's mind when they process information. I call this the Subconscious Encoding Process or SEP. Let us accept as the basis for our discussion that as humans we have two minds, the conscious mind and the subconscious mind. I like to think of them in this way.

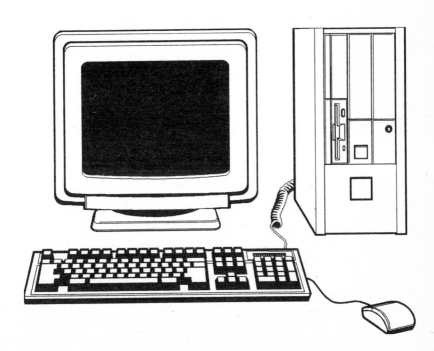

Just like a computer there is a screen, a keyboard, a central processor unit (CPU) and a printer or other output device.

If we consider the screen of the computer as our conscious mind and the CPU as our subconscious mind then it makes my explanation easy to understand.

The conscious mind, the screen, is simply the judge of the information that comes to us through our senses. We can think of this judge dealing with only one item at a time. It is said that the conscious mind can deal with seven items of information at a time. However, for our discussion and to maintain the analogy, we will consider that the conscious mind concentrates on just one item at a time.

The CPU is our subconscious mind where, like the computer, we store our memories. This does not judge information, it simply stores it.

Without taking the analogy too far we can think of the keyboard as our senses, i.e. the input device, and the printer as our mouths, i.e. the output device.

How can we use this information or analogy?

This is how it works.

When you ask someone a question they do not have a choice as to whether or not they answer that question. They may not verbalise their answer, but they always respond.

A simple demonstration would be as follows. Ask yourself the question 'Can you drive?' Your mind no doubt answered 'Yes' or 'No'. Imagine that you and I are having a conversation together and I ask you 'What colour are your eyes?' You either found the answer in your memory or responded 'I don't know.'

This is a simple but incredibly powerful concept. When we are saying 'Yes' in our minds we tend to move into positive attitude mode. When we are saying 'No' in our minds we tend to move into negative mode. Therefore the same must apply to others.

If we want the other party to our conversation to stay in positive mode we must phrase our questions so that Yes answers or positive mode answers are given.

Knowing this method or idea must prompt us to be particularly careful with the way in which we put questions to ourselves and others.

For example:

● 'You don't like blue then?'

Answer = NO, assuming for the moment that you do NOT like blue.

To phrase this in the positive would simply be:

'You prefer colours other than blue then?' Answer = YES.

I am sure that we have all had the experience in our lives of a group of young boys coming to our door on a Sunday morning, phrasing their question along the following lines:

● 'I don't suppose you want your car washed?'

Our answer usually . . . NO!

This happens because the 'Don't suppose' included in the question tends to prompt a No answer.

'I don't suppose you want to work this Saturday?'

'I don't suppose you want to tidy your room?'

'I don't suppose you would give me a raise?'

If we want others to say 'Yes' to our questions we can increase the likelihood of a positive response by the inclusion of what I call the 'Yes Tag'.

Among the 'Yes Tags' are:

| | | |
|---|---|---|
| Isn't it | Didn't it | Won't it |
| Won't they | Don't we | Wouldn't it |
| Shouldn't it | Hasn't it | Hasn't she |
| Haven't they | Can't you | Couldn't you |
| Aren't they | Doesn't it | Wasn't it |

There are hundreds of other examples that I am sure you can think of yourself.

These 'Yes Tags' can be included in questions to prompt a Yes answer. They have more impact if they are placed at the end of a question, although they can be at the start, middle or end.

For example:

'You will be able to stay to finish that report *won't you?*'

'You will be able to stay, *won't you*, to finish that report?'

'*Won't it* be useful if you stay and finish that report?'

'*Isn't it* a good idea to have that new computer system so that we can have instant access to the information we need?'

'It's a good idea to have that new computer system so that we can have instant access to the information we need, *isn't it?*'

'It's a good idea to have that new computer system, *isn't it*, so that we can have instant access to the information we need?'

I am certain that you have understood the principle of the 'Yes Tag' and with a bit of thought will be able to design questions that are relevant to your use . . . won't you?

We need to be careful with the use of 'Yes Tags' as, used too often, they make us sound as if we are using a technique. However, used sparingly, they can have great results. So, when we ask another person a question they have no choice as to whether or not they answer. They will always answer the question even if they do not verbalise their answer but use a facial movement, a body language gesture or a movement of their eyes instead.

If we want the other person to be positive we include a 'Yes Tag' to prompt a Yes answer.

Now let us look at the other side of the Yes or positive mode and examine what happens with a No answer and negatively phrased information.

By this I am not referring to someone who is negative about a situation – the person who always thinks the cup is half empty rather than half full, the person who sees difficulties in every opportunity rather than opportunities in every difficulty. I *do* mean the way in which our brains cope with negatively presented information.

The simplest example of this is the following test which you will be able to try with a friend or colleague.

Ask your friend to stand up and carry out your request. Then say:

'Please do NOT stand.' You will find that he or she will take a couple of seconds before sitting down.

Then repeat the test, this time rephrasing your request: 'Please sit down.' The person will do so much more quickly.

Here is another example:

'Please do NOT think of a blue elephant.'

Isn't that difficult to do? Why does this happen?

The reason is simple to understand. We have to think of standing to think of NOT standing. We have to think of blue NOT to think of blue and we have to think of elephants NOT to think of elephants.

If you want a situation where you want someone to sit down it is best to phrase your request 'Please sit down.'

By now it must be abundantly clear why we need to give a great deal of thought to the way in which we ask others to carry out tasks and instructions.

If you have children or know children you will recognise the following situations.

A child is asked to carry plates from the dining-table to the kitchen with the reminder 'Don't drop the plates!'

What happens in the child's mind? They have to think of dropping the plates in order to think of NOT dropping the plates.

A young boy is climbing a tree only to hear his parents say 'Be careful you don't fall!'

What does he have to do to think of NOT falling? He has to think of falling!

With very young children they will start to do exactly what

you do *not* want them to do before their young minds sort out the negatively presented information.

See a young child in front of the television set. The parents say 'Don't sit so close to the TV.' The child will move CLOSER to the TV before realising that the command was 'Move further away from the TV.'

## Self Commands

When we are attempting to persuade ourselves to undertake certain actions we also need to be aware of the effect of including negatives in that self talk.

For example, for a smoker who wants to give up smoking, saying 'I will NOT smoke' is in effect giving the brain a command that is difficult to obey. The mind receives the information as 'I will smoke, NOT', because in order to think of NOT smoking it is necessary to think of smoking.

For a person who wants to lose weight by not eating chocolate, it would be of little use saying 'I will NOT eat chocolate.' The mind receives, 'I will eat chocolate, NOT', simply because to think of NOT eating chocolate that person would automatically think of chocolate.

With all of those self commands or affirmations the requests need to be in the positive, focusing on the end result and not the area from which you wish to move. For example, the smoker would be better advised to say 'I will breathe fresh clean air, I take care of my body, I am healthy'; for the dieter, similarly, the phrasing would be better as 'I eat healthy foods, I eat salad and fresh fruit.' We need to concentrate on the result or outcome required.

With all of this conversation of persuasion, whether that be with ourselves by way of self dialogue or with others to create compliance with our requests, we have a much better chance of agreement if we phrase in the positive.

| | | |
|---|---|---|
| *Hang on tightly* | is better than | *Be careful you don't fall* |
| *Hold onto the plates* | is better than | *Don't drop the plates* |
| *Sit over here* | is better than | *Don't sit so close to the TV* |

Listen to your language and the language of others when dealing with children. So much of it is phrased in the negative.

Listen to the language you use with yourself and be careful to phrase what you say towards the results that you desire. It is far better to congratulate yourself on what you remember rather than chastise yourself for what you forget. It is far better to say, 'As I get older my memory gets better', rather than the usual societal mindset of 'As I get older my memory gets worse'.

## Subliminals

'Subliminal' means 'beneath the threshold of consciousness'. 'Subliminals' are governed by the idea that the conscious mind judges and the subconscious mind acts as the database for memory. The best-known example was the Popcorn Experiment, when an American cinema theatre inserted pictures of popcorn between the frames of the film that it was showing. What happened? At the interval the popcorn stand was inundated with customers wanting to buy popcorn.

All films provide similarly visual subliminal stimulus. The information we are receiving from the centre of the screen is received by our conscious minds. We make a judgement about that information before we store it. The information from the sides or edges of the screen bypasses our conscious mind and goes straight to our subconscious without judgement, thereby creating a much deeper feeling about that information. That is why when we see a film on the large screen it is more exciting, more emotional, more moving. The same film, seen at home on television, seldom makes the same impact. This is because on the small screen all the information is received by your conscious mind, judgement being made before storage in the subconscious.

Aural subliminal messages work in the same way. When we receive information straight to our subconscious we do NOT judge that information, we just store it and act upon it. This happens on subliminal message tapes by the message or programming being masked by white noise or a music sound-track. For example, subliminal assertiveness training tapes. Tapes without white noise or music to mask the message can be used as subliminals by simply turning down the volume of the cassette player until the noise of the environment acts as the mask.

As there is a great deal of controversy regarding the efficacy of subliminals, it is best to make up one's own mind on the subject.

## The Power of Questions

Let us move back to the idea of the power of questions within the Subconscious Encoding Process.

Imagine that you want to ask someone about his or her experiences. If you phrased the question 'Tell me something fascinating about yourself', most people would at first struggle to find an answer. This is because your style of question is asking them to access the whole of their life history database in order to provide an answer. However, if we ask the questions in the right order then it is much simpler for the other person to answer.

Let us go back to the analogy of the computer so that I can share this idea with you. Imagine that you are sitting at a computer, in front of its screen, and that the computer is running a Windows program.

On the screen will be icons, small pictures of the various main programs of that computer. Let us decide that one of those pictures or icons is the representation of the Sports file. To open that file we would double click on that icon and the program would run. Most likely a second set of icons would appear on the screen, in our example a number of sports such as basket-ball, golf, water sports. If we wanted to know more about golf, we would then double click on the golf icon to open that file, in which a list of golfing events might have been stored. From that file we might choose to open a document entitled 'Golf Pro' to extract the information we need.

This is PRECISELY the way we deal with a person's mind.

The 'double click' is the question that opens the file. When we ask a person a question, we know that they have to answer. If we make it difficult to answer by not opening the right file first, then the person may give us an answer that is not the one we want. The answer may simply have been the easiest one to find.

So if we want to know someone's experiences in their lessons with their golf pro, we would go about it like this.

Question 1   Do you play sports?   Yes.

The Sports file opens.

Question 2   What sports do you play?   Basketball, golf and water sports.

Now we know what files are there.

Question 3   Do you enjoy golf?   Yes.

The Golf file opens.

Question 4   Have you ever had lessons from a golf professional?   Yes.

The 'Golf Pro' document opens.

Question 5   What was the best thing the golf pro ever taught you?

You can see what we have done in this example. By asking questions in the right order we have made it extremely easy for the other person to answer. We have accessed the information we require.

Let us make this commercial. In business, when you have been dealing with a customer who is satisfied with the product or service you provide, you may want to ask that customer for the names of other potential customers. In the selling profession this is called 'asking for referrals'.

Many businesses survive on their ability to obtain referrals from their database of satisfied and happy customers. Other businesses never realise the opportunities for referrals that lie within their grasp. I like to think of referrals as the cheapest 'capture cost' lead we could ever obtain.

If we go about asking for referrals in the wrong way we diminish our chances of success to obtain them. The wrong way would be 'Do you know anybody else who could buy our products/services?'

What have we asked the customer to do? To access the whole of their business and life history database to try and find some names of other people who possibly might be interested in our company's wares. We are unlikely to succeed with that approach.

However if we structure the questions correctly and ask them in the right order then obtaining massive numbers of referrals is just so simple!

## How to Get Referrals

Imagine that you are the banqueting manager of a hotel at which a company has just run a successful conference.

I know that you will be able to translate this idea so that it is relevant for you and your business. However, in order for me to demonstrate the process, imagine that you are the banqueting manager.

You have been dealing with the sales director of the company that held the conference.

In conversation you would ask the sales director,

'Have you been in selling for many years?'

The Yes or No answer to this question will open the Selling file in the sales director's database or memory. It does not matter which answer is given. The file will still open. Next you would ask: 'I suppose that over those years you have met a number of other sales directors, haven't you?'

This question will open the Sales Directors document in the Sales file. The Yes answer is prompted by the use of the 'Yes Tag', 'haven't you?'.

Then you would ask: 'You'd be happy for me to send details of our conference facilities to some of them, wouldn't you?', the 'Yes Tag' again prompting the Yes answer.

Now you ask for advice, something that most people cannot resist giving, with a GENTLE assumption that the information we require will be forthcoming by saying: 'May I ask your advice?' After the Yes answer to that question, you would ask: 'Which of those sales directors do you think would be most interested to receive the information?'

If you accompany these words by taking out a piece of paper and pen in order to write down the names, the idea will work all of the time. Obviously the tones you use to deliver the questions must be conversational. You will need to personalise this idea to your busines; I can assure you that it works extremely well. Following exactly this method my business obtained 3000+ referrals in a three-month period.

### What Mode do my Questions Create?

Let us examine how the power of questions can have an impact on other conversations. You have bought a product from a large store and have a problem with your purchase. You return to the store, approach the customer-service desk and ask one of the customer-service staff: 'Do you deal with complaints?'

What mode will this question create? The COMPLAINTS mode.

Not the mode we would wish to create in the customer-service person's mind. If they move into complaints mode they are going to be ready for a battle.

It would be far better to phrase the questions as: 'I recently bought this item from your store and I wonder if you could help me?' This question will open the HELP file in the customer-service person's mind – a far better file to open than the COMPLAINTS file.

In a management or leadership role you may wish to obtain information from a member of your team.

Let us say, for example, that you are the manager of an administration team which interacts on a regular basis with members of the sales team. A classic 'us and them' situation in some companies.

You need information and could ask:

'What *problems* have you been having with the sales team recently?'

That question will open the SALES TEAM PROBLEMS file, so that your team member will think that you are looking for difficulties. We could, however, phrase the question in a different way in order to provide a more positive outlook and a more positive result:

'John, have you spoken to any members of the sales team in the last week?'

That question will open a file labelled Sales Team.

'What situations have arisen where you needed to *help* them?'

Note that we have focused on help not problems.

'What *solutions* could you suggest that would make those situations less likely to occur in the future?'

We have focused on solutions not problems.

You might think of it in this way: the problem and its solution are at either end of a straight line. When we are looking at the problem we cannot see the solution. When we are looking at the solution the problem has disappeared.

**Problem** . . . . . . . . . . . . . . . . . . . . . . . . . . . . .**Solution**

So let us return to our central theme. The Subconscious Encoding Process.

Scientists say that we remember everything we experience. Problems occur not with memory but with recall. Knowing this means that when we wish others to remember what we have said we need to take care in the way in which we present our information.

## The Six Keys for Retention

### 1. Firsts

### 2. Lasts

We tend to remember the first and last items in any situation. For example, I am certain that you can remember your first day at your place of work and no doubt you can remember the last day. You can probably remember your first girlfriend or boyfriend and no doubt remember your last boyfriend or girlfriend, perhaps the person you married.

However, you may not be able to remember all the boy/girlfriends in between the first and last and certainly would be unable to recall all the days in between your first and last days at your work.

When giving a presentation to a group try to be the first or last person to speak.

### 3. Unusual Items

We tend to remember things that are unusual.

You can imagine a situation where you went into a restaurant and sitting at the bar was a man dressed in a luminous green suit with a red cape and wearing a pale blue hat.

You would be able to describe him years later simply because his dress was so unusual. If you are making a presentation to a group of people and wish them to remember what you say, make certain that you are unusual in your approach. Perhaps have large coloured cards with the key thoughts of your presentation to hand out. Perhaps have slides with unusual or funny drawings.

Use as many creative ideas as possible to make your presentation unusual. It will then be more easily remembered by that group.

## 4. Linking

If information presented to us has some connection with things we already know, then we will remember the new information more easily. This is how humour works. Imagine a comedian telling a joke about golf. For those who understand the game, the joke will contain humour. For those who have no knowledge of golf the joke will fall flat. When giving information ensure that it links into something that the recipient already knows. Or, to put it differently by using the analogy of the computer, open the right file and then put the new information into the file.

Here is an example (simply answer the questions in your mind as you read them):

Question 1   Have you ever walked on a tightrope?
Question 2   Have you ever seen a tightrope walker?
Question 3   Did you know that it was in June 1859 that
        Blondin walked on a tightrope across the Niagara Falls?

The process was as follows.

The first question opened your tightrope walker's file in your mind. The second question ensured that the file was wide open and the third question installed the information regarding Blondin, June 1859.

This uses the idea of linking information to that already known. You would already have some knowledge of tightrope walking, even if this was just seeing a tightrope walker at a circus.

## 5. Repetition

Things that are repeated again and again tend to stick in our minds. Most of us learned our multiplication tables by rote, by simple repetition.

Imagine that you have come home late one night. Having arrived at the front door of your house, you realise that there has been a power cut. All the lights in the house are out. You would not wait at the front door until it was daylight, you would enter your house and move around with confidence. This would happen because the way around your house is a well-trodden pathway of memory in your brain. It is the repetition of information that helps to stick the data in the database. That is why it is so important to open the right file in order to extract information.

In a presentation situation you can make use of this fact by summarising regularly throughout the presentation and then finishing with a major summary of the information you have given.

## 6. Enthusiasm

When we are enthusiastic about information we remember it.

If you have children of school age you will relate to the following. You see your children late in the afternoon and ask them what they had for lunch. Often they cannot remember, even though it was only a few hours before. However if you ask them the names of the players of their favourite team they WILL know them all. If you ask them the names of the latest hero figures they will know all the details. This happens because they have an enthusiasm for the subject.

With presentations ensure that you are enthusiastic about the information you are giving, thereby transmitting enthusiasm to the audience.

So when you are giving a presentation, whether to a large audience or just a few people, you will ensure that what you said is more easily remembered if you:

(a)  are the first to speak
(b)  or the last to speak;
(c)  have your main points at the start and end of your presentation;
(d)  make the presentation unusual;
(e)  link information into the audience's mind by opening the right files first;
(f)  repeat on a regular basis;

(g)   be enthusiastic and create enthusiasm in the listeners;
(h)   use the power of questions both actual and rhetorical;
(i)    use 'Yes Tags' to prompt Yes answers;
(j)    prepare and practise the questions before the presentation;
(k)   summarise the main points at the end of the presentation.

## Predicting the Answers

Let us have some fun with some more questions. There is a serious intent with these questions as they will enable us to examine what happens in someone's mind when questions are asked and answered.

If you do not come up with the same answers as the ones I suggest, try the questions on your friends and colleagues to see what happens in other people's minds.

You will need to imagine that I am asking you the questions and then answer them in the order in which I ask them.

- Will you please choose a number from 2 to 9?
- Will you now multiply that number by 9?
- You now have a two-digit number in your mind.
- Will you add those two digits together?
  (i.e. 26 = 2 + 6 = 8)
- You now have a single-digit number in your mind.
- Will you please subtract 5 from that number?
- We have a code for the answer you now have, as follows:

If you have 1 as your answer will you translate it into the letter A?
If you have 2 as your answer will you translate it into the letter B?
If you have 3 as your answer will you translate it into the letter C?
If you have 4 as your answer will you translate it into the letter D?

Now that you have a single letter in your mind, please answer the following questions:

Will you think of a **COUNTRY** beginning with that letter?

Will you think of an **ANIMAL** beginning with the **second** letter of that **COUNTRY**?

Will you think what **COLOUR** that **ANIMAL** is?

Will you think of how many **LEGS** that **ANIMAL** has?

Most people would have the answers:

**Denmark, Elephant, Grey** and **Four**.

If you didn't, then try the questions on friends and colleagues. I am certain that you will find, as I have found with thousands of people on communications skills seminars, that most people do have those four answers. Let us examine what was happening with those questions.

(a)  All numbers from 2 to 9 when multiplied by 9 produce a two-digit number; when these digits are added together the answer is invariably 9.

$2 \times 9 = 18 \qquad 1 + 8 = 9$
$3 \times 9 = 27 \qquad 2 + 7 = 9$
$6 \times 9 = 54 \qquad 5 + 4 = 9$

(b)  Subtracting 5 from that *known* 9 answer will produce 4.

(c)  The code translation will ensure that the mind of the listener is holding the letter D.

(d)  Then we come back to the idea that everyone has files in their mind where they store information.

The first of the four questions was: Will you think of a Country beginning with that letter? Now, as I already knew that the letter was D, the real question was:

Will you name a country beginning with D? Most people come up with the answer Denmark.

The second question was really Will you name an animal beginning with the letter E? I knew that there was a good chance that you had E as the letter because it was likely that you had Denmark. The second answer is usually Elephant, in which case the question of what colour and how many legs is fairly simple.

I have used this example with thousands of people and over 90% have the answers Denmark, Elephant, Grey and Four.

Let us try another example to continue our examination of the files in people's minds.

Question: Will you please think of
A colour?
A flower?
A piece of furniture?

Now please turn to page 217 to see if your answers coincided with mine.
Did you give the same answers? Many people do simply because on the top of their colour, flower and furniture files are those particular items.

Question:   Did you do Latin at school?
Question:   Can you, using one line, make this six?
IX

The answer is on page 217.

What was happening in your mind if you were unable to make the connection? The first question, 'Did you do Latin at school?', was answered by your mind. It did not matter whether you answered Yes or No. Your Latin file opened and while you were in that file you may have missed the possibility of using the S.

Question:   How good are you at mental arithmetic?
Imagine you are driving a bus between two major cities. There is no one on the bus. At the first stop 5 people get on the bus. At the next stop 6 people get on and 3 people get off. At the next stop 9 people get on and 2 people get off. At the next stop 3 people get on and 8 people get off. At the next stop 6 people get on and 1 person gets off.

Now answer the following three questions:

- How many people are on the bus?
- How many stops were there?
- What was the name of the bus driver?

Answers are on page 217.

If you were unable to answer the third question, this is what happened in your mind. The first question, 'How good are you at mental arithmetic?', pushed you into what is called Left Brain Mode. The left brain in right-handed people deals with Logic, Language, Linguistics. Remember that it did not matter whether you answered yes or no, you still accessed your mental arithmetic file. While you were in left brain mode, you may have missed the start of the journey which stated: *Imagine* you are driving a bus. That word *imagine* is a right brain function and you may well have missed it while locked in left brain mode by the first question.

And now a final question in our examination of how peoples' minds work.

Question:   Do you have a good imagination?

Now will you please answer the following questions?
    What is 1 + 1?
    What is 2 + 2?
    What is 4 + 4?
    What is 8 + 8?
    What is 16 + 16?
    What is 32 + 32?
    What is half of 64?
    What is half of 32?
    What is half of 16?
    What is half of 8?
    What is half of 4?
    What is half of 2?

Question:   Now will you name a vegetable?

Turn to page 217 for the possible answer.

If you answered with the stated vegetable it was because you created that picture in your mind with the adding and subtracting.

If you had a different vegetable it was simply that you created a different shape in your mind. Again, my suggestion is that you try these questions on your friends and colleagues and see how many give the same answers as those I have suggested.

What we can realise from these fun questions is that we all do have files in our mind and that the analogy of the computer is valid. This fact must make us think very carefully about the questions we ask during our conversations. We are now also aware that when we give information to others they are more likely to remember that information if we open the files in their minds before we install the data.

## Visualisation

We will now examine the effect of visualisation and how we can use that effect to produce results in communication.

Some years ago an experiment was carried out with basketball players to discover the effect of visualisation on their practice sessions and subsequent skill.

The team of players was divided into three groups, A, B and C.

Each was tested on the penalty shot at basketball to create a starting point of skill.

Then the teams were asked to do the following:

Group A was allowed to practise for one hour a day for a three-week period.

Group B was asked to undertake NO practice for a three-week period.

Group C was asked only to VISUALISE practice for one hour a day for a three-week period.

The results were astonishing.

A fresh test of skill on the penalty shot showed these results:

Group A (Actual Practice) had improved by 2%.

Group B (No Practice) had deteriorated by 2%.

Group C (Visualisation) had improved by 3.5%.

A staggering 150% increase over Group A, the group that had actually practised!

This seems to be the explanation:

Our brain/mind cannot tell the difference between vivid imagining and reality. The memory pathway is the same, whether the activity is vividly imagined or actually under-taken.

There has been – and continues to be – so much research in this area proving the effects of such imaginings that we must begin to accept that visualisation does work.

For example, athletes have for some years now visualised themselves running their races . . . and winning. The same techniques have been used by those who throw the javelin to a new personal best distance, downhill skiers who visualise successful completion of the course. They actually see in their mind's eye their name in first place on the giant electronic scoreboard.

Many personal development trainers, myself included, have taught visualisation in the process of goal setting. If we visualise ourselves as having accomplished our goals, the results are successful. Perhaps the best expression I ever heard in this connection was from an American author, Dan Lee Dimke, when he said:

**'Let us live our lives as though all of our dreams had come true and then challenge reality to catch up.'**

The idea of imagining reality is now used in many learning situations. One rapid reading course I have taken includes a self-hypnosis tape based on visualisation of action. The process works as follows:

- Sit quietly, breathing deeply, and imagine a clock in your mind. It matters not if you can see the clock, hear the clock or are simply aware of its existence.
- Make the clock say, for example, 10 o'clock.
- Start practising the skill you wish to improve, seeing

yourself or feeling yourself or hearing yourself undertaking the activity at the skill level you require.
- Practise for a little while.
- Look back at the clock and note that one hour of time (by THAT clock) has passed by. This will probably take only about five minutes.
- Count from 1 to 10.

The results can be amazing. Skill levels increase as though actual practice had taken place. If you have a skill you wish to improve, try this method and see the results for yourself.

Relaxation courses teach the same idea. Finding the clock in your mind and relaxing for one hour by THAT clock, then feeling as though you had relaxed for an hour in *real* time.

I remember running an in-house personal development and sales course for a company in the south of England. I had noticed and remarked on the fact that one of the delegates was left-handed. 'I have always thought it would be good to be able to write left-handed,' I said. 'Why don't you try then?' was the left-hander's response.

So I did and, using visualisation and actual practice of one hour per day real time and one hour per day mind time, I achieved remarkable accuracy and speed of left-handed writing in just one month.

Well, all this is fascinating 'stuff', but how does it help us with conversation and persuasion?

In fact this knowledge makes a tremendous difference to the way in which we speak and the things we say to others and ourselves.

This is how it works.

What I am about to share with you is an extremely simple concept that can sound complex. It will take time for you to personalise the idea and use it in your business and social life. As it is a **technique** it may sound manipulative. It is! However, I believe that the difference between manipulation and motivation is in the intent of the user. If we use any idea of persuasion to influence another person's thought process we could call that manipulation. It depends on the end result we are seeking. If the intention is a win/win situation, we are using motivation. If the intention is win/lose, we are using manipulation.

## The YARD Technique

I shall explain the basic concept before telling you what the acronym means. If we are able to implant, by statements and questions, information into someone else's mind and then ask a question about that information, we will know what answer is likely to be given. In fact, we can almost predetermine what answer we want.

It may be worthwhile re-reading the above paragraph.

Let me give you an example of the idea.

Let us for the moment pretend that you are in the computer business and that your role in that business is to introduce new clients to the hardware, software and computer-training courses that your company provides.

In a meeting with a potential client you would explain what happens over time when someone places an order with your company.

- The order is placed.
- The installation engineers arrive on the customer's site to install the wiring system for a network computer system.
- The hardware and software are delivered and installed.
- Those who are to operate the system attend **Part I** (an important item) of the training course that your company provides.
- Those who have been trained now use the system for three months.
- Those who use the system attend **Part II** of the training course.

This is easy to explain and would be understood by anyone.

Obviously the various items can only take place sequentially and that is critical to the method.

When you, in your role of computer executive, are absolutely confident that the potential buyer fully understands what happens and when it happens in time, you could then . . .

ASK A QUESTION THAT COULD **ONLY** BE ASKED ONCE MOST OF THOSE SITUATIONS HAVE COME TO PASS.

For example:

Let us say that two teams of ten people each will attend Part I and Part II of the training course.

During the first conversation with the potential buyer you could ask:

'Will you keep the team together or mix them up for Part II?'

You can hear and see what has happened with that question.

If someone answers a question that could **only** be answered after a certain series of events have taken place then you can be fairly certain that in their mind those events **have** taken place.

If you then, in the above example, ask the other person **IF** they want those events to take place . . . they will access their database and answer YES.

This concept of the YARD. Technique must not be confused with a standard assumptive question, it is far more powerful than that.

The acronym YARD stands for

Y   Yes
A   Action
R   Result
D   Delighted.

For those in a selling role the process is:

The order has been placed (Yes).
Delivery has taken place (Action).
The customer has paid (Result).
The customer is pleased with the purchase (Delighted).

For those in a non-selling role the process is:
An agreement to take action (Yes).
The action has taken place (Action).
A result has happened (Result).
The other party is pleased with the result (Delighted).

Having taught the YARD Technique to a number of people on sales courses I know that the concept is easy enough to grasp. Some people, however, have experienced difficulty in working out questions that fit the technique. In order to work out your questions this is what to do:

- Imagine a situation where you want to obtain an agreement. This may be a sale, an agreement for a certain action to take place, an idea accepted by your colleagues, certain actions by your children, spouse, suppliers or customers.
- Visualise the fact that the action has taken place, that you have your agreement.
- Ask yourself what question you would normally ask at a second meeting with this person that you could honestly ask at the first meeting.

The answer to that self question will give you the questions that will fit into the YARD technique.

# 3     Reaching Home Base

Over the next few chapters I want us to move forward and look at what's been said about eye movement and the different types of language that people use in their everyday conversations.

This subject of eyes and language is extremely interesting and I know that it will have you looking far more intently at and listening even more actively to everyone you meet.

Television news will take on a whole new dimension. Listening to anyone being interviewed in any situation and being a third party to any conversation will become a fascinating and revealing experience.

It will be as though you are able to read what people will say even before they say it.

## The Home Bases of Language

It is said that modern man is able to communicate ideas with a vocabulary of approximately 4,000 words. Within that word bank we each have a home base of language which we prefer to use, reflecting the way in which our brains and minds deal with information.

Let me explain. Can you imagine having a conversation with a person from a foreign land? We will assume that your native tongue is English and that the native tongue of the other person is French. It would be easier for the

French person to understand your message or communication if you translated what you had to say into French. With that we could all agree, providing that your translation was skilful.

However, within each native language everyone has their own home base of language. Back in 1972 two scientists, Richard Bandler and John Grinder, discovered the idea of home bases of language and created what has become called Neurolinguistic Programming or NLP.

Having now utilised the idea of matching another person's home base in order to build rapport with that person, I can report its effectiveness. It is one of the simplest and most effective ways of enabling another person to understand clearly whatever we are trying to communicate.

An expression used in NLP – The Map is not the Territory – sums up the concept brilliantly.

If you and I were together in a room with 100 other people, a large room in a hotel, and we were all asked to leave the room and then write a description of that room, we would NOT be surprised that those descriptions varied from one person to another. Some of that crowd would describe the 'look' of the room, others would describe the 'feel' of the room and still others would be concentrating their descriptions on the acoustics or sound of the room.

We all have our own perceptions. In other words, while the room would stay the same (the territory) the descriptions (the map) would be different for each person. The MAP is NOT the TERRITORY.

If we are able by skilful listening to understand someone else's map and use the language of the map, we will enable that person to understand clearly what we have to say. In the process we will also create rapport with that person. He or she will feel as if we are on the same wavelength.

There are five main home bases of language, though most of the population, in my experience, falls into two of the top three home bases. The five are:

| *Home Base* | *Language Base Used* |
|---|---|
| Visual | Seeing |
| Auditory | Hearing |
| Kinaesthetic | Feeling/Touching |
| Olfactory | Smell |
| Gustatory | Taste |

It is important to note that WE ALL USE ALL OF THE HOME BASE LANGUAGE WORDS. WE SIMPLY HAVE A PREFERENCE FOR CERTAIN WORDS WHICH TEND TO FALL INTO ONE HOME BASE. That home base is our map.

Before we examine the three main home bases of Visual, Auditory and Kinaesthetic, please carry out the following exercise.

Imagine that an eccentric millionaire had given you £100,000 and that the only stipulation was that you had to spend it on a car. Decide on which car you would buy and three reasons why it would be that car.

(a) The Car would be . . .
(b) Reason 1 . . .
(c) Reason 2 . . .
(d) Reason 3 . . .

Let us examine some of the possible answers and into which category or home base they may fall.

Words and phrases such as 'shape', 'colour', 'it would make me LOOK good', fall into the visual category.

Words such as 'safe', 'fast', 'roomy', 'feel', would be kinaesthetic words.

Phrases such as 'the stereo system would be great', 'I would like what people would *say* about me', would fall into the auditory category.

If I haven't covered the reasons you gave, then try to decide into which category they would fit. If you have words such as luxury, quality, economical etc., then ask yourself the question: 'Why is that important to me?' and keep asking 'Why?' until you hear yourself use one of the home base words.

Before we go any further let me explore with you a number of the words used in the three main home base categories.

| Visual | Auditory | Kinaesthetic |
|---|---|---|
| See | Hear | Safe |
| View | Listen | Movement |
| Picture | Harmony | Touch |
| Look | Noise | Comfortable |
| Observe | Rings a bell | Explore |
| Watch | Heard | Fast |
| Behold | Discordant | Handle |
| Spy/Vision | Music to my ears | Grip |
| Spectacle | Sound | Feel |

Let me repeat at this stage that we all use words from all of the home bases, however we do have a preference for words from one home base.

Moving back to the idea of the car. Picture (there is my visual language) this situation. A customer goes into a car showroom, intent on looking at or perhaps even buying a new car.

The sales person in our example has not been exposed to the information about home bases of language. The sales person has a home base of visual language and the customer has a kinaesthetic home base. Just see how much mismatched language there is in the following mock conversation.

CUSTOMER: I *felt* that it was about time to change my car.
SALES: I *see* what you mean.
CUSTOMER: I want something that is *fast* but also *safe*.
SALES: Have a *look* at this one.
CUSTOMER: Um, that has a *smooth* finish on the body work.
SALES: Yes, it *looks* great, doesn't it? I can just *see* you in this.
CUSTOMER: Can I *get in* and *feel* what it is like to drive?

SALES:   Yes, I can *see* your friends *watch* you drive up in this one.

CUSTOMER:   I can't quite get to *grips* with it. I'll *explore* what else is on the market.

SALES:   OK. I *look* forward to *seeing* you again.

CUSTOMER:   I'll be in *touch* when I am ready to *move* ahead.

You can clearly see what has happened, albeit obvious that I have created the conversation to demonstrate the mismatch. If you listen carefully to other people you will soon hear their home base.

Let us examine what could happen if the sales person understood the concept of home bases of language and took the time and trouble to listen to the customer and reflect the home base.

CUSTOMER:   I *felt* that it was time to *change* my car.

SALES (hearing the 'felt'):   Great, good of you to *come* to us. I *feel* that we can probably *find* what you need. What were you thinking of *getting*?

CUSTOMER:   Something that *goes fast* and still *feels safe*.

SALES:   Here, *jump* into this one and **see** how it *feels*.

CUSTOMER:   It *feels* great!

SALES:   Would you like to *drive* it?

CUSTOMER:   Sure, let's **see** how it *goes*.

You have the idea I am sure. You will also have noted that the customer and the sales person used some words that were not in their home base. That is because we do not avoid all words that are not in our own base, we use words from all the home bases. We just have a preference for one home base.

If we take the time to listen carefully to the content of someone else's language and then match his or her home base we will build massive subconscious rapport.

When I started this chapter I wrote 'I want us to *move* forward and *look* at what's been *said* about eye movement and the different types of language that people use in their everyday conversations.' You will note that I have used words from all three of the main home bases. This was to ensure that my message was as clear (visual) as possible for anyone.

Here are two more examples.

One partner is visual, the other is kinaesthetic. The visual partner has just arrived home to find the house in an untidy state.

> VISUAL PARTNER:   *Look* at this place, what sort of *sight* is this for me to *see* when I come home?
> KINAESTHETIC PARTNER:   It *feels* all right to me, it's *comfy!*

One partner is visual, the other is auditory. They are out buying a stereo for their home.

The visual partner will want something that *looks* good, that will match the *colour* scheme of the lounge. The auditory partner will be concerned with the *sound* quality of the system.

All of these mismatches of language can create problems and arguments. Now that is not to say that you have to marry or be in partnership only with someone who has the same home base. It does, however, prompt us into being aware of the home bases of the important people in our business and social lives.

There are other ways of spotting the home base of other people.

Visual   Tend to speak quickly.
   Are often the standard body shape person (mesomorph).
Kinaesthetic   Speak more slowly than visual people.
   Are often the slim body shape (ectomorph).
Auditory   Speak more slowly than kinaesthetic people.

In commercial matters or at your place of business it would be as well to know the home bases of language of the main people in that area. The boss, the team players, the suppliers, the customers, the banker or accountant.

We will diminish our chances of success in conversation if we mismatch the language of others. For example, imagine asking the boss for a raise and totally mismatching the language.

The boss is visual and we are auditory.

'*Tell* me, boss, what do I need to do to have a raise?'

We should be saying '*Show* me.'

Instead of saying 'When will I *hear* your decision?', we should be saying 'I *look* forward to your decision.'

I remember some years ago talking to a customer of mine about an in-house audio programme for a team of salespeople. I had sent the director of the company a copy of one of my programmes. As the programme was from a series of tapes of fifteen titles, two tapes in each title, the cassette box looked somewhat like a video box.

I called the customer and asked if he had listened to the tapes.

His response was 'Sorry, Peter, I haven't had a chance to LOOK at them yet.' I thought perhaps he believed it was a video, so I made the point that the box contained two audio tapes. 'I know,' was his reply, 'I just haven't had a chance to look at them yet, I'll see if I can look at them this week.'

Why would this director use the word LOOK in connection with audio tapes? Simply because his home base of language was visual.

The next chapter will continue our discussion on home bases of language and incorporate the way in which people move their eyes and the massive amount of information we can learn from those movements.

# 4    The Eyes have It

It has always been said that the eyes are the windows to the soul and I have certainly found that eye movements are the clearest indicator of someone's thought processes.

Research has indicated that we have two halves to our brain known as the Left Brain and the Right Brain.

These two halves deal with different types of data.

**The Right Brain** deals with intangibles, spatial awareness, colour, music, pictures, rhythm, imagination, daydreaming and patterns.

**The Left Brain** deals with language, logic, numbers, sequencing, analysis, mathematics and what we might label academic thought.

The above descriptions are for most right-handed people and some left-handed people. As people use their brains their eyes also move.

The diagram is of a right-handed person. What is on the right of the diagram as you see it is therefore that person's left side.

Looking up and to their left indicates that they are accessing visual memory.

Looking up and to their right indicates that they are creating visual information.

Looking to the left side, towards the left ear, indicates that they are accessing hearing memories.

Looking to the right side, towards the right ear, indicates that they are creating sounds.

Looking left and down towards the left shoulder indicates that they are engaging in self talk, self dialogue.

Looking right and down towards the right side indicates kinaesthetic thought.

Looking up and into the middle distance indicates that the person is engaging in self talk.

## Right Handed Person

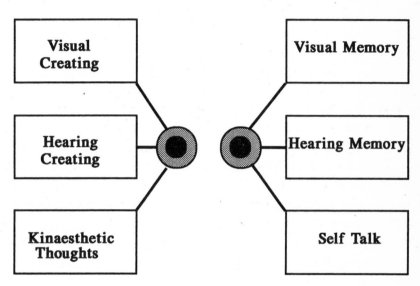

The simple way to remember this information is to make the connection that when someone looks LEFT it is because they LEFT the information in their memory.

To prove these movements to yourself ask yourself the following questions and feel the movements of your eyes.

1   Think of a journey you undertake regularly. How many traffic lights do you go through on that journey? Or how many roundabouts or islands do you go round?

   Did you feel that your eyes moved up and to your left (up and to the right if you have a left-handed brain!) to access your visual *memory*?

2   Now (on the assumption that you do NOT have a pale green suit with purple stripes and white spots), what would you

look like in a pale green suit with purple stripes and white spots?

Did you feel your eyes go up to the right to *create* the picture?

Try these other questions regarding accessing clues with other people. You will be surprised how much movement takes place. I have found that the best practice to get used to this idea is to be the third party to a conversation, perhaps even watching someone being interviewed on television.

I am absolutely certain that if you have not known this information before you will be astonished to see how easy it is to spot these movements.

Let us try some other visual accessing questions.

1  What is the colour of the carpet in your lounge?
   You should access up and left as you find the memory of the picture of the carpet and its colour.
2  Assuming that you do not have blue chairs in your lounge, what would blue chairs look like in that room?
   You should have felt your eyes move up and right as you create that picture.


## Auditory Accessing Questions

As for visual accessing, for most right-handed people the memory will be on their left and the creating on their right. The movement of the eyes for auditory access will be sideways towards the ears. Answer these questions and feel the movement of your eyes.

1  Can you hum, in your mind, your favourite piece of music?
2  When was the last time you heard someone say your mother's maiden name?
3  When was the last time you spoke to your best friend?

These questions should have had your eyes move towards your left ear if you remembered the information needed to answer the questions. If your eyes moved up and left, you may have accessed a picture of the event in which you heard the information.

Please ask yourself these auditory creating questions.
1   What would people at work say about your skills?
2   If you made up an advertising jingle for ice cream, what would it sound like?

You should have felt your eyes move towards your right ear. The creating sound eye movement.

I am certain that you are now starting to feel the different movements of your eyes.

Now try some kinaesthetic questions.
1   Think about holding a piece of cotton wool.
2   Think about weighing a bag of sugar in your hand.

Did you feel your eyes move down and to the right, towards your dominant right hand? If that was the case you were thinking in kinaesthetic mode.

So when we ask someone a question and see their eyes move in a distinct way we will know in which manner they are accessing.

## Summary

People have a home base of language.
    The main ones are Visual, Auditory and Kinaesthetic.

The different body shapes are:
    Mesomorph   The person with a compact and muscular build of body. The shape I call the standard body shape is often visual.
    Endomorph   The person with a soft, round body and a high proportion of body fat sometimes uses gustatory (taste) and olfactory (smell) words in their language.

> Ectomorph   The person with a lean, delicate build is often kinaesthetic in language.

Over many years of watching and listening I have found that over 60% of the people I meet are visually based, about 35% are kinaesthetically based and only 1% are auditory based. You will find out by listening carefully the percentage points in your own group of people.

Matching another person's home base will build subconscious rapport and enable the other person to understand your messages more clearly.

As a matter of further interest when someone puts their nose in the air and looks down and right they are probably accessing their gustatory or olfactory bases.

Some left-handed people access in exactly the opposite manner from right-handed people, i.e. to the right for memory and to the left for creating.

## Eyelid Movements

The movements of the upper and lower eyelids are very good indicators of another person's thought processes.

### The Upper Eyelid

The level of the upper eyelid indicates someone's interest in the situation in which they find themselves. This may be their level of interest in what you are saying.

> **Position 1**   When someone's upper eyelid level is in this position they are showing shock or surprise at what has happened or what has been said. This position is when the white of the eye can be seen above the iris (the coloured part of the eye).
>
> **Position 2**   When someone's upper eyelid level is in this position they are indicating HIGH interest in what is happening or what has been said. This position is when

the upper eyelid is between the top of the pupil (the dark centre of the eye) and the top of the iris.

**Position 3** When the upper eyelid is in this position, the person is losing interest. This position is when the upper eyelid is across the centre of the pupil.

**Position 4** Someone indicating this upper eyelid position is either bored with the situation in which they find themselves or may have even fallen asleep!

You can understand how useful this information will be to you.

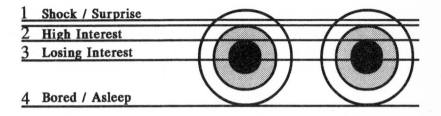

1 Shock / Surprise
2 High Interest
3 Losing Interest
4 Bored / Asleep

You are giving a presentation to a small group of people at work and you want to know how receptive they are to your information. Careful watching of the upper eyelids will tell you everything you need to know. If you find that the eyelids of one of the group has fallen below the high interest level then change your style. If you are sitting, stand up and continue from the new position. Write something new, shocking or unusual on your flip chart or overhead projector. Or ask that person a question. All of these actions will see their attention re-focused.

## The Lower Eyelid and Inner Canthus

In the corner of the eye at the side of the nose is a red triangular part called the inner canthus. The showing or hiding of this area can be a clear indicator.

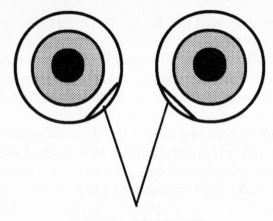

## INNER CANTHUS

When the inner canthus is visible then the person is showing a degree of interest. When the inner canthus is covered the person is showing concern or even disagreement. The inner canthus is covered by a movement of the lower eyelid being pushed upwards and towards the nose. Try the movement for yourself and feel your mind move into 'critic' mode.

I suggest that you never ask for another person's agreement when you cannot see their inner canthus. Ask questions to uncover the reason why they are giving out this signal. When their lower eyelids have relaxed, that is the time to ask for that Yes or agreement.

For example, let us say that you are explaining to your team manager or team leader your thoughts on the re-organisation of the office.

As you are making your point about moving certain parts of the office, you see relaxed lower eyelids with the inner canthus clearly visible. When you say 'This will mean moving John Smith to a different section as we will not need him anymore on our team', you see the manager's face take on a completely different look. The lower eyelids have moved and covered the inner canthus. At this point you need to ask a question before continuing with your presentation and ideas, a question to find the problem. You might say 'I haven't finished explaining all of the ideas. However, what do you think so far?'

The manager responds: 'Well, it's not bad, but I am concerned that we will not have a place for John Smith.'

You might respond: 'I have given some thought to that and have been to see Sheila in Accounts. In general conversation, without mentioning my plan or John, Sheila says that she is looking for another person and I think that John would fit the bill.'

Perhaps instead of asking a question, when you saw the lower eyelids cover the inner canthus, you might have said 'I have given some thought to John's position and I know that there is a position in Accounts that would suit him down to the ground.'

If the concern is with John's position in the company and the Accounts position is as good as you say it is, then that lower eyelid will soon relax, showing the inner canthus once more.

You will appreciate that I have simply given an example of watching the inner canthus. I use eye watching a great deal in my commercial and social activities.

It does take practice to be able to watch other people's eyes without appearing to stare at them. However, like all of our skills, repetition is the master of skill.

## The Pupil

The dark centre of the eye, the pupil, is a clear indicator of a person's level of interest in what they are seeing, hearing or feeling.

When the pupil dilates, the person is showing a degree of interest or excitement in what they are hearing, seeing or feeling.

When the pupil contracts, the person is indicating a concern or lack of interest.

As we are all aware, the light of the surroundings also changes pupil size, so great care must be taken when reading pupil sizes.

I am given to understand that in ancient China, when spectacles were first worn, traders had a dark piece of crystal put in the centre of their glasses. This was to prevent other traders seeing the change in the pupil size when interest was shown and known to be harder in the negotiation on price.

**PUPIL SIZE**

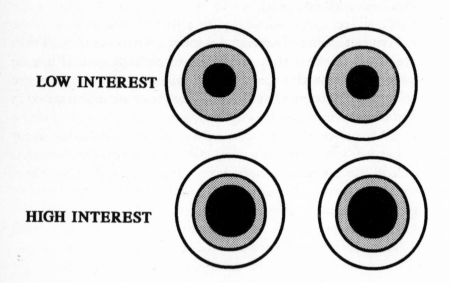

LOW INTEREST

HIGH INTEREST

## Where to Look

As eye contact is such an important part of communication and conversation we will now examine *where* to look at another person.

When talking to others we like to see their eyes in order to gauge the reaction our words are having. No doubt you have experienced having a conversation in a car. It is so difficult to speak without being able to see the eyes of a person sitting in the back of a car while you are in the front. What do we do? We turn round or, if driving, try to catch the eyes of our listener in the rear-view mirror.

Comic heroes all have some form of eye power. One of the best-known examples is Superman, with his X-ray vision and the ability to burn anything just by looking at it!

When giving presentations we need to give eye contact to

everyone in the audience. In small groups this is easy to do. Gazing at each person for about five seconds at a time as we make our presentation. In larger groups it is sufficient to look at groups of people, each of whom will feel that you made individual eye contact.

We all feel uncomfortable with a person who will not make eye contact. When that person is talking we feel as though they are unsure of what they are saying or perhaps even telling an untruth. When that person who will not make regular eye contact is the listener, we feel as though they are uninterested in what we have to say.

As a listener therefore we need to make eye contact for about five seconds at a time on a regular basis. If making eye contact is difficult for you then simply look at a spot between the eyes of the other person. From anything but a short distance the other person will not be able to tell that you are not looking directly into their eyes.

## The Business Look

If our gaze is centred around the triangle formed by a person's eyes and mouth then that look is indicating that we are interacting on a fairly formal basis, the business look.

## The Social Look

If our gaze is moving around a triangle formed by the other person's eyes and the centre of the chest then that look indicates that we are interacting on an informal basis, the social look.

## *The Intimate Look*

If our gaze is moving around the whole of the other person's body, we are looking them 'up and down' and we know that we are giving out a completely different message.

In a face-to-face conversation it is possible to indicate to the other person that you are uncomfortable with their presence or wish them to end the conversation or leave by gazing at the middle of their forehead.

## Summary

1   The eyes are the windows to the soul.
2   The eyes show the way in which a person is accessing his or her brain.
3   The direction in which the eyes look indicates either access of memory or creation of pictures, sound and feelings.
4   The upper eyelid is a clear indicator of interest or lack of interest.
5   The lower eyelid covering the inner canthus indicates concern.
6   Pupil size indicates changes in interest by dilating and contracting.
7   Eye contact should be approximately five seconds at a time.
8   Be aware of where you are looking at other people.

# 5    Questioning Skills

The next areas we are going to examine are questioning skills and opening questions. By *opening* questions I do not mean *open* questions. We will cover open and closed questions in Chapter 8.

The first question we must ask ourselves is 'Why are questions so powerful?' Well, as we know, questions are always answered and therefore we are able to create a number of different situations and reactions by the types of question we use.

## Basic Types of Question

### 1. Information Questions

A question enables us to give out information as well as receive information. There are two distinct forms of this type of question.

#### (a) Implied Information
*Example:*
Let us say that you work in the sales administration department of a company that supplies cement to small building contractors. One of the sales team has asked you to process an order for 20 bags of cement. You know from your own knowledge and records that the customer usually places orders for 10 bags of

cement. Just in case a mistake has been made, you speak to the sales person concerned and ask: 'Do you want me to send 20 bags of cement to ABC Builders? They normally have 10 bags.' The question has two possible answers: Yes, in which case a larger order than normal has been taken; No, in which case the sales person will be pleased that you spotted the error.

The implication of the question is NOT that the sales person made a mistake. It is simply that you are *giving* information regarding the usual order of the customer. The tone of voice used in asking this question is all important. We would not use a 'know it all' tone of voice.

*Example:*
Your manager has prepared a new form for customers to use. You have read the form and think that people will be confused by it. Instead of making the statement 'This form will confuse people!' you would turn it into a question: 'Do you think that some customers may be confused by this part?' You have made your point in a far smoother way.

## (b) Stating Information

The second method by which we can give information is an extremely powerful one and returns our thoughts to the Subconscious Encoding Process, which we discussed in Chapter 2. First state an item of information and then ask a question. When the question is answered the information preceding it has been accepted.

The format is statement/question.

**When the question is answered the statement isn't questioned.**

This, which I can only call a technique, is used a great deal by political interviewers and advertisers. Statement followed by a question.

Most politicians seem to have been taught to spot the technique in action and will question the statement before answering the question – that is, if they answer the question at all!

*Example:*
'People tell us that our training courses have their sales people doubling their results within just three months' (the Statement). 'Do you think that we advertise that fact enough?' (the Question). You can see what would happen with this type of question. When the question is answered, the statement is NOT questioned. And, most importantly, it does not matter whether the answer to the question is Yes or No! Once the question is answered, the information that came before it has been taken in by the listener.

*Example:*
'This job will involve us in about six hours' overtime' (the Statement). 'Do you think that the team would prefer to do it this week or next week?' (the Question). Regardless of the answer, 'This week' or 'Next week', the information that the job will take six hours' overtime has been accepted by the listener. This is a far more powerful idea than the closing technique called the assumptive close. The difference is that the information is given *within* the question.

Knowing that you now understand the technique (the Statement), how would you be able to use it in your job? (the Question).

## 2. Focusing Questions

Questions can focus people on the potential outcome of a situation and make them think about that outcome.

*Example:*
In a meeting where diverse views are being expressed and the meeting is dragging on with no apparent end or agreement in sight, a question such as 'What do we all want as the outcome of this meeting?' will clearly focus others on the end result for which we are searching.

*Example:*
When trying to decide if your company should or should not go

ahead with the purchase of a piece of equipment, you would ask:

'What are we trying to achieve by buying this product?'

*Example:*
A self question to focus our own thoughts could be:
'Where do I want to be in a year's time?'

*Example:*
When someone is trying to persuade you to their point of view, you could ask:
'How do you think I will benefit by accepting your idea?'

*Example:*
In a buying role a buyer could ask a sales person:
'What are the two main benefits of your product to our company?'. Similarly, a sales person could ask a buyer:
'What do YOU see as the two main benefits of our product to your company?'

This question will tell the sales person or the buyer the other's main points of interest. If the home bases of language have not been uncovered at this stage, it is likely they will be revealed in the explanation of benefits.

### 3. Silence Filling Question

A good question can fill the embarrassing silence that can happen in conversations and start a fresh direction for talks.

*Example:*
In an interviewing situation, the interviewer could ask the interviewee: 'What questions would you like to ask me?'
This may open up areas of interest that the interviewee wants to put across.

*Example:*
In a performance appraisal, the head of department could ask the assistant:

'If you were me, what questions would you like me to ask you?'

*Example:*
In a meeting, the person running the meeting could ask each person in turn:

'What one thing would you suggest we do that would increase sales, increase profits, decrease costs, make production run more smoothly?'

## 4. People Problem Questions

Questions can bring people together when there are difficulties in a relationship.

*Example:*
A mediator between two team members or two family members could ask:

'What are your shared goals for this situation?'

'Which of the solutions we have already discussed do you think would be acceptable to the other party?'

'What outcome would be good for all of us?'

*Example:*
When dealing with a member of your team at work, you could ask:

'What do you see as the differences in our needs and how do YOU believe that we could come to an agreement that was acceptable to both of us?'

*Example:*
If you are in a sales role, a suitable question might be:

'What additional information can I give you that would enable you to make a decision?'

## 5. The Listening Question

Questions can indicate to another person that we were listening actively. We have already examined active listening in Chapter 1 and you know that Level 4 of active listening is the ability to answer questions. It clearly indicates to another that we have been listening if we ask good questions.

*Example:*
'Bill, a few moments ago you said that . . . How does that fit in with what you just said about . . .?' (we are not trying to catch Bill out with this question).

*Example:*
We could ask: 'Am I right in thinking that what you are saying is . . .?'
   or
'I think I understand what you mean. Could you give me another example so that I am sure all is clear?'

   If you have a complaint, it is vital to ensure that the other person will listen to you actively. One of the best methods I have ever learned about complaining is to express your views in three stages:

- I am not happy.
- This is why I am not happy.
- This is what will make me happy.

Most people when complaining only state that they are unhappy or annoyed with the product, service or situation. They then say why they are unhappy but seldom, if ever, go on to suggest a solution.

   If you have the need to complain, state the fact that you are unhappy, state why you are unhappy (all in a calm voice) and then continue by telling the other party what will resolve the situation to make you happy again.

   I have used the idea for many years and had so much success with it that I share the idea with as many people as possible. Using this method makes it easier for both sides. I have had hotels change my room and offer a free bottle of wine with dinner. Car companies have sent a member of staff for my car and have left a loan car free of charge. There have been so many successful outcomes. Please use this method to complain. It works.

## 6. The Calming Question

Questions can have a remarkable calming effect in difficult situations. If you have young children you will know that it is quite easy to distract them when they are upset or angry by asking them questions. This works because questions have to be answered. With adults questions can also have a calming effect.

*Example:*
You work on the customer-service desk at a large store. A customer approaches and is really annoyed about a product they have bought from your company. In a calm tone of voice, once they have had their say you ask:
'On behalf of the store I apologise for the mistake.' (the Statement). 'Tell me, what do you wish me to do to correct the problem?' (the Question).

## 7. The Rapport Question

Questions enable us to build good rapport with another person. Rapport can be defined as being a harmonious and useful relationship with another. We have examined using other's home bases of language to build rapport. We have taken the time and effort to translate our messages into their language in order to help them understand more clearly what we are saying. Now questions can play their part.

*Example:*
Questions such as 'How may I help you?' said in the right tone can build rapport. This should not be asked in a sing-song voice rising at the end of the sentence!

Any question that shows other people that you care about them and your relationship will create rapport.

In a work environment asking about someone's relatives,

providing you really wish to know, shows that you are interested in them and their lives.

Asking clients or suppliers about things that were discussed at previous meetings creates rapport. This links in to my thoughts on active listening and taking notes. Keeping good records is a marvellous aid to future conversations.

So, questions are really powerful. They can give implied or actual information. They can make others think. They can focus minds on the outcome of any situation. They can fill an embarrassing silence and prompt fresh conversation. They can bring people together, prove that we are utilising our active listening skills, have a calming effect and create rapport.

If questions can do all that – and they can – then it is no wonder that we think of them as powerful tools in our box of conversation skills.

## Mistakes made with Questions

### 1. The Wrong Tone of Voice

If use the wrong tone of voice when we ask our questions, they do not usually have the desired effect. I wonder if you remember the film *Pretty Woman*, starring Richard Gere and Julia Roberts?

Julia Roberts, dressed in her 'street' gear at the start of the film, enters a high-class dress shop only to be asked by the assistant 'Does Madam think that she is in the right shop?' The tone, let alone the question, said it all!

Mind you, it was amusing to see Julia Roberts return to the same shop later in the film, dressed very differently, to be met with an oh so different response.

The tones we use must be appropriate to the question.

### 2. Asking a Question and Not Listening to the Answer

Some questions are asked only out of so-called politeness and the answer is ignored as self talk comes into play. Use the Rapid Repeat Method to listen actively, as discussed in Chapter 1.

### 3. Manipulating Questions

There is a fine line between manipulation and motivation. I have covered before my thoughts that techniques used to create an outcome can be manipulation and that it is the INTENT that makes the difference.

### 4. Questions into Monologues

I am sure that you have been at meetings where someone has used the opportunity to ask a question that turns into a monologue on his or her views on the history of mankind and the meaning of life. This should be avoided.

### 5. Asking the Wrong Questions

Failing to listen actively often results in asking a question when the answer has already been clearly stated. This does not create a good impression.

### 6. Not Asking a Question

Sometimes it is obvious from a person's tone of voice that he or she meant to ask a question but end up making a statement. In the majority of situations, questions are much better starters, continuers and finishers of conversations than statements will ever be.

## Practical Applications

We are now going to discuss the different types of question that we can use in a variety of situations, whether business or social.

### 1. The Leading Question

This is where the answer is given in the question. Politicians are great users of the leading question.

*Example:*
'Wouldn't you agree that our policy on housing is producing results?'

This is a front-loaded 'Yes Tag' question as well as being a leading question.

*Example:*
At court hearings, which are familiar to many of us through dramatised versions on television, we often hear 'Your Honour, counsel is leading the witness.'

What's happening? The counsel is asking questions with the answers loaded into the question, so that the witness can simply confirm the facts stated in the question rather than give facts.

Market researchers say that the results of opinion polls are determined by the questions asked in those polls.

It was once asked, in an opinion poll, whether a certain American politician was right to use his family connections to avoid the military draft. What a loaded question that is! How could anyone other than the staunchest supporter of that politician agree that he was right to use his family connections in that way? However, according to the results of that poll, 93% of the people asked said that Mr X was *wrong* to use his connections to avoid the military draft.

If we use leading questions we should give a great deal of thought to the effect that the question will have on the listener. If the listener believes that we are using a leading question on purpose, we will instantly lose credibility and break rapport.

## 2. Phrasing the Question

The phrasing of questions is all important. Perhaps one of the best stories to illustrate the point is the following:
Two men go into a church and ask the priest questions.

JACK:    Father, is it alright to smoke while I am praying?
PRIEST (*emphatically*):    No!

JOHN: Father, may I ask your advice?
PRIEST: Certainly, what is it you wish to ask?
JOHN: Is it alright to pray while I am smoking?
PRIEST: Yes, of course it is!

The point is well made. We need to give a great deal of thought to the impact our questions will have and the likely response based on the way in which we phrase them. You will have noted that, as in the example of 'How to get referrals' explored in Chapter 2, I have used the question 'Please may I ask your advice?' This is an extremely powerful question and is almost guaranteed to receive a Yes answer. I cannot remember a single occasion in my life when anyone has ever answered No to this question.

## 3. Interviews and Appraisals

In job interviews and appraisals we should avoid using leading questions as it will prompt the listener to tell us what we want to hear.

*Example:*
'This job requires someone who can type at 3,000 words per minute. How fast can you type?'
   We all know what the answer would be!
   'This job requires someone who loves to meet new people. Do you like to meet new people?' The reply: 'Oh, yes, I *love* to meet new people.'
   'This job requires someone who would be prepared to wear training shoes with a suit to work. What do you think about that?'
   We would not be surprised at the answer.

Interview questions and appraisal meeting questions should open up the other person's mind and have him or her giving information on which to base a hiring or action decision.

*Examples:*
'When did you leave your last job?'
'How did that come about?'

'What would your previous manager say were your best strengths?'
'What would they say were your lesser strengths?'

It is necessary to ask questions that are both easy to ask and easy to answer, questions that do not give away too soon what you may be looking for in a candidate. Further questions can be asked later in the meeting, once you have established that the candidate may be suitable for the job.

In interviews and appraisals as well as in day-to-day conversations there are times when we need to be certain that the other person is telling the truth. Later in the book, in Chapter 7, we will discuss lying in greater detail.

At this stage, however, let us look at the *two-stage question* which can be used to probe for accuracy during interviews.

To make the method clear let me explain it in this way:
   Question 1:   What is 9 – 5?
      We know the answer will be 4.
   Question 2 (asked later in the same conversation):   What is 5 + 4?
      We know that the answer should be 9!

In an interview this *two-stage question* would be:
   Question 1:   What did you do before you worked for ABC?
   Answer: I worked for XYZ.
   Question 2 (later in the conversation):   What did you do after you worked for XYZ?
   The answer must be, if the truth is being told, I worked for ABC.

The best way to design questions for interview and appraisal meetings is to start at the end and work backwards. By that I mean decide on the information you require and build a series of questions that will enable you to uncover that information.

This will take time. However, it is time well spent.

It is effective use of the six Ps Principle:
   ***Proper Planning Prevents***
   ***Particularly Poor Performance***

## 4. Soft Expressions

Soft expressions incorrectly used can rob our conversations and presentations of power. While these words and expressions have their place in our language they should never be used by default.

### (a) Tone
The tone we use can take emphasis and power from our words. If we use an apologetic tone with weak words, we are unlikely to make an impact with our conversation. We are less likely to be able to persuade others to our point of view.

### (b) I'm sorry to bother you but . . .
It may well be that you are sorry to bother someone. However, those words do nothing whatsoever for what follows them:

'I'm sorry to bother you, boss, but may I have Thursday off?'

### (c) I may be wrong but . . .
### I'm perhaps being unfair but . . .
These two expressions set up the listener's mind to believe that you are being wrong or that you are being unfair. They should be avoided unless that is the feeling that you wish to create.

### (d) If you like
This expression used at the end of a sentence usually diminishes the strength of the sentence.

'I need you to stay late on Friday, if you like'

### (e) Filler Words
We are all no doubt guilty of using such filler words from time to time. Uh, um, you know, right, OK, if you know what I mean, well err . . . If we can avoid them, however, our messages will be much more clear and concise.

### (f) Misplaced Emphasis
Misplaced emphasis can detract from the content and distract the listener's ear.

Such, really, surely.

'It's really important that we get this finished today.'

'Surely you mean . . .'

The *Airplane* film of some years ago starring Leslie Nielsen focused clearly on the common use of 'surely': 'Surely you can't mean . . .' 'Yes I do mean that and don't call me Surely!'

### (g) Maybe, Sort of, Like

'Maybe it's a good idea to . . .' would be more powerfully expressed. 'It's a good idea to . . .'

'It's kind of a good idea to . . .' would be more powerfully expressed 'It's a good idea to . . .'

### (h) Don't you think? Isn't that so?

'Don't you think that we should . . .' is better phrased as 'We should . . . '

All of these soft expressions do have their uses. It is their overuse or misuse that robs our conversations of impact.

In a study done with managers it was found that a mixture of hard and soft expressions produced the greatest rapport and understanding with their people. Soft expressions in abundance made the people think that the manager was a soft touch. Overuse of hard expressions had people treading too warily to be able to perform at their best. They were frightened to put a foot wrong.

To have the best effect on people, particularly if you are a management or leadership role, use a mixture of hard and soft expressions with a mixture of hard and soft tones.

## 5. Work Discussions

Often in a work environment we can be asked by our manager or director to undertake a certain task with the rider that the task has to be done NOW!

This NOW may cause disruption to the other jobs and tasks we have in hand. This is how to deal with such a situation. Remember that a question is far better than a statement. The correct tone of voice must also be used.

- Which of my current jobs should I leave to do this new one?
- So that I can get this new job done on time, can somebody else help me with my other jobs?
- I can't get it done by Monday with the current work schedule, would Wednesday be OK?
- I have a number of jobs on at the moment, could you tell me how this job fits into the prioritisation of those others?

All of these questions focus on the fact that you want to get the new job done and that there is a challenge to meet in order to accomplish that fact.

The converse of being asked to do things is when you want things done. We can divide this into three main areas:

- by your director or manager;
- by a co-worker;
- by a subordinate.

### (a) Business Superior

With a director or manager it would be as well to focus his or her mind on the fact that something else needs to happen once the relevant business superior has carried out the task you want done.

*Example:*
'In order that I can get this report done by Wednesday (Statement) will you let me have that information by Monday?' (Question).

### (b) With a Co-worker
*Example:*
'I need that information by Wednesday, will you give me your answer by then?'

As an additional thought, I have always found it far more effective to add an exact time by which you need action.

## (c) With a Subordinate
*Example:*
It is best to use a slightly stronger voice than usual when making specific requests.

'Will you give me that information by 2 o'clock on Monday?'

## 6. The Leadership Role

When we are acting in a leadership role we need to give careful thought to our way of dealing with our team members.

Very often 'we' language rather than 'You and I' will create a better effect and result.

You can imagine a team leader starting a meeting as follows: 'What *you* all need to do is to put in more effort. *You* are simply not performing at the level *I* would expect, what are YOU going to do about it?'

What a terrible start to a meeting. That would create resentment immediately and the likelihood of a productive meeting has been greatly reduced.

However if the leader were to start with 'We' language, a much better result is likely to be produced.

'We need to make a decision *together* as to how *we* can increase the results of *our* team; the recent analysis showed that *we* were falling behind. What suggestions can *we* come up with to improve *our* performance?' This approach would have every one working together as a team to solve the team's problems, each individual feeling that his or her contribution was worthwhile.

You have probably been to meetings where the boss or team leader started:

'I've made a decision to . . . and I need your opinion.'

It is rather like the leading interview question, 'This job needs someone who can type at 3,000 per minute, how fast can you type?'

The answers to either of these would not surprise any of us.

Starting with 'I've made a decision . . .' is unlikely to receive any worthwhile input.

It would be far better to rephrase it as a request:

'*We* need to decide on *our* course of action regarding . . . please give me your input.'

## 7. The Team Leader's Mistake

A mistake often made by directors, managers and team leaders is in the area of prizes for achievement. I have known many situations in which managers and leaders have decided to set a goal for their team members, be it in production, administration or sales, with a prize to be awarded for accomplishing the goal. Sometimes the prize set is NOT one that the team members would like to win. It is based on the manager's thought of what they would like to win. When the team members have no interest in winning the prize, this can have a demotivational effect, with everyone doing their best NOT to win.

I recall doing some training for the telesales team of a major computer company. The average age of the team was about 22. The manager of the telesales department had set goals for the whole team and the individual prize for the highest performer was a weekend at a local high-class hotel. There was valet parking, a swimming pool and health club. Dinner and dancing . . . the whole works.

The telesales team confided in me that they did NOT want to win!

I asked them why.

Their reason, which was valid for them, was that none of them were used to dining or staying at such a high-class hotel. They felt that they would be embarrassed by not having a new car for the parking attendant to park. They were unsure which knife and fork to use at dinner and were even concerned about what to wear for breakfast.

Now this is not to criticise the telesales team members in any way. They were young people who simply had no experience of hotels. The mistake the manager made was in not asking what they would like to win if they achieved the goals set. The second mistake was setting the goals and announcing them rather than involving the team in the goal-setting exercise so that they would 'buy in' to the goals.

When I asked the team what they would have liked to win if they had hit their target, their reply surprised me as I am sure it would have surprised their manager. A £25 voucher for a national store was all they wanted.

This would have cost the company far less money, produced better results and had the telesales team committed to success.

In a management role it is far better to talk to the team about the potential competition, get feedback, let the team know why we want or need the competition and let them decide on the prize for achievement. Invariably they will ask for a prize costing far less than you might have expected.

## 8. When Things Go Wrong

All of us find ourselves in a role of having to deal with a situation when things have gone wrong. These are some of the ways to deal with that situation.

Our focus should be on WHAT went wrong not WHO was wrong.

You can picture the situation. You are the manager of a department. You see your people in a huddle; whispered conversations are taking place. Purposefully you stride over to find that there is a problem.

'Who did this?' could be one way to start the conversation. The result would be sheepish looks all round.

Perhaps it would be better to ask, in a gentle tone, 'What happened?'

What we really want to know is WHAT happened and WHAT has to be done to rectify the situation. Blame, if blame is necessary, can come later.

In that excellent book *The One Minute Manager* the basic rule quoted for dealing with people is **Catch your people doing it right!** Do not catch them doing it wrong.

I firmly believe that whatever we recognise in others is what they will repeat.

*Recognition = Repetition*

If you focus on what they did wrong, what happens? They do it again!

Give a dog a bad name and it will be a bad dog. Many parents inadvertently follow that rule when they say to their teenage children:

'You never tidy your room.' What happens is that they will not tidy their rooms, they will live up to their parents' expectations. Sure enough, the result of repeatedly hearing 'You are always late' will be that the children are indeed always late.

## 9. Chastisement and Praise

If we have to criticise another person adversely, it is far better to criticise the action rather than the person who carried out the action. Similarly with praise, it is far better to praise the action rather than the person. Praise of a person rather than their actions often sounds like flattery and is far too sugary to sound like honest praise.

Adverse criticism is best carried out in private.

- Explain what has happened as you understand the situation.
- Ask for comments. Remember that you are focusing on *what* went wrong.
- Explain the consequences of the action.
- Remind the person that you appreciate the good things they do.
- Ask them to keep doing those good things in future.
- Wait for their affirmation that they will keep doing good things.
- Shake hands.

This final point, shaking hands, may sound obvious. If this stage is missed, however, the effect of the meeting is greatly diminished.

This is a far better way of handling adverse criticism than saying:

'You are hopeless, I might have known you would get it wrong. Can't you ever get things right? I don't know what I'm going to do with you!'

That 'You' and 'Blame' language will never resolve the problem. Instead, the principle of Recognition = Repetition will have been firmly implanted in the other person's mind.

Let us always remember when it comes to chastisement and praise that we treat people as human beings and not human doings!

# 6  Starting a Conversation

We all know that when we meet someone the first words that are usually said are 'How are you?' The most frequent response is 'Fine.' This is so automatic that it is hardly worth saying at all.

My ideas on this response are, to say the least, a little unusual. Having shared them with thousands of people and having had such positive feedback, however, I know that you will also experience positive results.

F I N E could stand for Feeling Inwardly Negative Everyday.

I am sure that most people don't feel negative when they say 'Fine'; they just say the word out of habit.

However if we give a positive response to that oft-asked question 'How are you?' then we start every conversation on a much more positive note.

For some years now I have been using 'Tremendous!' and although in cold print this may appear a little over the top, in reality it has a 'Tremendous' effect.

People are stopped in their tracks because they are expecting 'Fine' or 'Not too bad' or 'OK.' The unusual response is such an interruption of the established pattern of conversation that it creates an instant smile on the face of the other person.

Now I am not suggesting that you use only 'Tremendous', but an upbeat word of some description really can help.

Having learned this idea at my seminars, people have reported back to me that they have started using such strange expressions as 'Cosmic', 'Wonderful', 'Marvellous' and many others, all to good effect at the start of their conversations.

Some years ago a senior manager from one of my in-house clients attended an open seminar I was holding. When I had finished making my point about responding in this way, he asked if he could say a few words. I said 'Yes, of course', although I was unsure *what* he was going to say.

He stood and told the other delegates that I had carried out some in-house training at his company for over 100 of their staff and that if he had to say what one thing had made a difference to the attitude in the company it would be this idea of positively responding to 'How are you?'

Now I'm not quite sure what this says for the other training I did for them! However, it certainly was an excellent confirmation of the power of such a seemingly silly and simple idea. One group I know and have trained now use a different word for each day of the week. Marvellous on Mondays. Tremendous on Tuesdays. Wonderful on Wednesdays. Thunderous on Thursdays. Fantastic on Fridays.

I urge you to try almost any word other than fine and see what responses you receive.

## Conversational Approaches

When we start a conversation with another person we are attempting to do a number of things. The following ideas will be relevant for different situations.

1   The first thing we are trying to do with our conversation opener is to break the other person's preoccupation with whatever they may be doing in order that they are able to listen actively to what we have to say.

*Example:*
You go into an office where a colleague is working on a report. She invites you in, looks up and says in an enquiring tone 'Yes?' Now you know that the report on which she is working is

uppermost in her mind. A quick decision needs to be made as to whether the matter you want to talk about is more important than that report. Whatever words you utter in the next few seconds will definitely need to break your colleague's preoccupation with her report.

2    The opening words may need to make the other person want to listen.
3    You may want to excite the other person.
4    You may want to put the other person at ease.
5    You may want to make the other person feel important.

Certainly at an interview or appraisal meeting you would want to use an opening that would put the other person at ease and feel comfortable before the interview began.

We know that the first words we use must set the scene for the whole conversation.

*You never get a second chance to make a first impression!*

So, how are we going to do that? How are we going to start our conversations with those whom we already know and with those we don't know?

*A stranger is only a friend we haven't yet met!*

If we care about the people with whom we interact – and I'm sure that you do – we must take the time and effort to plan our openings. This is not being too structured or using a technique, it is caring enough to bother to take the time and effort required. If the meeting with another person is important we would take time to plan the meeting.

Imagine that the next meeting you are to have was to be the last meeting you could ever have and that the whole of your future success or financial security rested on that meeting. How well would you plan? How well would you prepare your opening and the questions you were going to ask? Obviously very well.

I remember some years ago listening to an audio tape where the presenter was talking about openings for sales people. He said: 'Imagine being charged with a crime you did not commit. If the barrister who was to defend you said "I don't bother with any planning or practice I just walk into court and say 'Hi Judge!' and then I just wing it on the day", would we want THAT person to defend us? I doubt it!'

So our openings must be planned for the start of any important conversation.

This is as simple as sitting down with a pen and piece of paper and deciding what you want as the outcome of a meeting. As described earlier, it is best to work backwards from that outcome to the start.

*Examples:*
You are to have a meeting with your manager and you want him or her to agree to a change in the current working procedures of your department.

'I think that we have a problem, can I see you for a few minutes?' is definitely not a good way to start.

'John, I have an idea to increase the efficiency of the department, when would you have time to discuss it?' would be much better.

When planning our openings we need to give thought to why the other person would want to listen to us. We may need to include a reason or an incentive or a benefit for the other person within our opening few words.

'I think that we could save a substantial amount of money if we changed the operation of the office' (Statement). 'When would you have time to discuss it?' (Question). 'I think that we could make a substantial amount of additional profit if we . . .' (Statement). 'Have you time to discuss it now?' (Question).

'How interested would you be' (Question) 'in reducing the amount you spend on your . . .?' (Statement with implied benefit).

'If there was ever a way that we could cut our costs on . . .' (Statement with implied benefit), 'how interested would you be to hear the details?' (Question).

The same principles apply if you are to have a meeting with a supplier.

'Bill, your people are really messing up. This latest delivery was three days late, for the second time this month.'

This may have a result, but a much better way to begin would be: 'Bill, I need to talk to you about how WE speed up deliveries. Do you have a moment now?'

Next, it is a good idea to write down the openings that you are thinking of using for important meetings.

Some people are concerned that if they write down the words they are going to say it will make them sound wooden or lacking in spontaneity. I believe that the reverse is true!

Many sales people would be violently opposed to writing a script for professional use, stating the reasons:

- It will make me sound as if I am reading from a script.
- I will not be able to react to what the customer says.
- What will I do if the customer doesn't follow the script!

In fact we all tend to have a script in our minds for conversations that we hold on a regular basis. Listen to any one who works with a telephone – and that's most of the population – and you will hear them say the same words with the same tones and inflection again and again.

If we think of actors in a play, they have a script. They know precisely what they are going to say and yet it doesn't make them sound wooden. In fact quite the opposite is true. Knowing the words we will use enables us to concentrate on HOW we will say the words.

Now I know that the other actors in the play have the same script. However, that does not invalidate the idea. Knowing the possible directions which a conversation may take and having given thought to our potential answers or statements ensures that we are properly planned.

For important conversations we should practise our openings. It is important to give thought to how we will deliver our opening lines, what tones we will use, how quickly we will speak.

In any conversation and persuasion situation we need to obtain the other person's name right at the start of that conversation.

## The Cocktail Party Syndrome

The 'Cocktail Party Syndrome' states that people respond more quickly to their own name than to any other sound. In a crowded room, with the babble of conversation all around us, we would still hear someone say our name.

If we haven't obtained or have immediately forgotten the other person's name at the start of a conversation, we will be unable to use that name to prefix what we want to say.

Why does it happen so often that, having been introduced to someone, we immediately forget the name?

Well, usually because we are not paying sufficient attention at the moment of introduction. We are caught up in our self dialogue or just waiting to speak. We have only heard the name once and therefore create only a once-trodden memory pathway.

However, we can lock that name into our memory so easily if we do the following:

You are introduced to, say, John Smith. Immediately repeat his name in your mind. Then look at the person's face and fix it in your mind by repeating the name aloud in a questioning tone: 'John Smith?' You will receive an immediate Yes answer. Then follow with 'John, good to meet you.'

Using this method you will have heard the full name, John Smith, twice and the first name, John, three times in the space of a few seconds. There is now a far better chance of locking that name into your memory bank than if you had heard it only once.

When I am introduced to someone for the first time I also try to find some feature of that individual's face that begins with the same letter as his or her first name. These help to fix the name in my mind.

*Examples:*
You meet a man called Bob. He happens to have a bald head and is a large man. You can think of him as 'Big Bald Bob'!

You meet a lady called Tina who is tall and tanned. You could think of her as 'Tall Tanned Tina'.

Making the connections amusing helps to enhance the memory and subsequent recall of this important piece of information.

There are so many excellent memory courses these days, both in book form and on audio cassettes, that if this is a problem area for you I suggest that you obtain one and learn the techniques they contain.

If at all possible, within a few seconds of hearing someone's name, use it again. If the surname is unusual ask the person to spell it. This alone can prompt some interesting conversations regarding the origin of the name. This will definitely be an area that most people are easily able to talk about.

Using a person's name at the start of a conversation or question is a guaranteed way to get that person's attention. It will also make sure that he or she will listen to what you have to say.

*Example:*
You've been introduced to John Smith.

As the conversation proceeds you turn to John Smith and ask:

'What's your opinion about . . .?' or 'John' (then a slight pause as John focuses on you), 'What's your opinion about . . .?'

If we are able to hear someone's name clearly, then lock it into our memory by whatever method we choose, we avoid the embarrassment of forgetting. I am certain that this has happened to you. Your host introduces you to someone, then moves away to talk to someone else. There you are having a conversation with someone whose name you cannot remember. That is bad enough. However, what is even worse is when someone else you know joins you and looks at you expecting you to introduce the person you're with. You can't do it!

All of this embarrassment can be avoided by simply taking a few seconds to focus and lock in the new person's name.

## Smiling and Enthusiasm

The next important parts of any conversation are smiling and enthusiasm. We are all more likely to talk to people who approach us with genuine smiles on their faces and enthusiasm in their voices. Unfortunately so many people walk around with a downturned mouth or frown on their faces and boredom in their voices.

Smiling is contagious. When we smile at someone, the chances are that they will smile back at us. The world really is a mirror.

If we are able to be enthusiastic about what we have to say, not so over the top that people think we are trying to 'hard sell' them something, then others will be only too pleased to have conversations with us.

I remember some years ago working for an American company called Diversey. There were 300 sales people in the United Kingdom and I was one of them. I worked in their catering division, selling cleaning chemicals to hotels, public houses and commercial kitchens. Our sales meetings were held in a room at a service station and one evening my sales manager introduced the team to a new product Diversey was launching. The product was an oven cleaner – not something that many people would get particularly excited about. However, the sales manager was tremendously enthusiastic about this new product. He told us that when you spread the green 'gunge' on an oven that hadn't been cleaned for many years, you simply had to leave it for ten minutes to do its work. You then wiped off the gunge and the accumulated dirt of grease of years would come away and the oven would look brand new.

We were sold! During the next few weeks we sold more of the oven cleaner than when we had the product to demonstrate. This wasn't because the product didn't work, far from it. Like all of the Diversey range it worked. It lived up to its claims. No, it was that we sold on one thing alone – enthusiasm!

People love to talk to someone who is enthusiastic, as long as that enthusiasm is appropriate to the situation or circumstances. We can help create enthusiasm in another person by using one of the ideas we covered in Chapter 2, the Subconscious Encoding Process. We simply get the other person to say Yes.

This is easy to do and has someone's conscious mind holding a positive thought. In a face-to-face meeting, when you are introduced simply repeat the other person's name with an enquiring tone in your voice and emphasis on their surname. 'John **Smith**?'

The other person, John Smith in this example, will ALWAYS say Yes!

When you are making a telephone call it is easy to get two Yes answers.

*Example:*
You call a company and ask for the manager of the Bought Ledger Department. The telephone is answered 'Bought Ledger Department, Deborah Evans speaking.' You say, with an enquiring tone and emphasis on the surname, 'Deborah **Evans**?' Deborah will say 'Yes'. You continue with 'The **manager** of the Bought Ledger Department?' In her capacity as manager, Deborah again answers 'Yes.' Two, easy to obtain, Yes answers at the start of the conversation, putting the other person in a positive mode to receive the rest of your communication or message.

## Meeting New People

There are times when we wish to meet new people and there isn't anyone to introduce us. The first thing to do at a social or business gathering is to look for someone who may want to have a conversation. This we would easily pick up from people's body language.

If a person is standing, looking down, avoiding eye contact with everybody, he or she is clearly saying 'Don't talk to me!' If someone is standing or sitting with arms or legs crossed, looking bored, then again they are indicating that they do not want to be approached.

Unfortunately we often see these poses and body language gestures used by company representatives at exhibition stands, saying to all the world 'Don't come to my stand, I don't want to talk to anybody.'

So the first thing to look for is someone who wants to talk.

However, what words are appropriate to start those conversations?

We can concentrate on three areas:

- The other person;
- Ourselves;
- The situation in which we find ourselves.

The simplest ways are:

- State a fact, then ask for an opinion.
- Follow a statement with a question.

The fact states something with which the person can agree because the fact is obvious. The request for an opinion immediately involves the other person in the conversation.

The statement gives information and again the question which follows the fact involves the other person in the conversation.

*Example:*
You find yourself in the coffee break at a seminar or Parent – Teacher Association event and see someone to whom you would like to talk.

Saying 'It's cold for this time of year!' is likely to receive the response Yes or No. It would be far better to say, 'There must be over two hundred people here. What prompted you to be here today?' or 'There must be over two hundred people here. What's your involvement with this event?'

A fact or statement followed by a question, often a request for an opinion.

Here are some other ideas for conversation starters:

- Start with a question about your hosts:
  'Mike and Diana have certainly invited a large crowd. How do you know them?'
- Start with a fact about yourself:
  I'm with ABC Company. We are in computers. What's your involvement with today/this event?'
- Start with a fact about the other person or their situation:
  If you are walking down the road and see a neighbour in their garden, you may want to start a conversation with them.
  'That's an excellent lawn. How do you manage to keep it so green?'
  Very few people will answer with 'I water it!'
- I've always enjoyed talking to someone who is a (teacher, priest, salesman, doctor etc.). Tell me, how did you become involved in that? How did you get started? What made you go into that line?'
- 'That was an interesting thing you just said about . . . Why do you think that?'
- 'Weren't you at . . . ? (Mary's party or the Conservation Group meeting or wherever you saw the person last). What's your involvement with today's event?'
- 'I've always been interested in . . . (computers, for example). You seem to know a lot about them. What impact have they had on your job?'
- 'I've always been interested in the . . . profession. How do you start in that?'

In order to receive clues as to what to talk about to another person, listen to what they are saying in general conversation.

Some years ago I was at a party in the south of England and heard another person speaking in a northern accent. I opened the conversation with 'Bill, your accent's a long way from home, how come?' to which I received the following reply:

'The force moved me when I broke my leg!'

You can imagine the possibilities that opened up for more conversation. 'Which force? How did you break your leg? Where did they move you from?'

Here are some other conversation opening possibilities which you will be able to customise:

- I wonder what would happen if . . .?
- Can your present 'X' do 'Y'?
- How important is it that . . .?
- Wouldn't you agree that . . .?
- Isn't it true that . . .?
- Isn't it your experience that . . .?

You will recognise that many of these are front-loaded 'Yes Tag' questions and you may receive a one-word answer, in which case you may need to ask further questions to continue the conversation.

We need to be as creative as possible when we give thought to our commercial and social openings.

I once heard of a man who was in sales in the life insurance industry. He experienced problems when he told people what he did because they all thought that he would immediately try to sell them insurance. In order to create better situations and conversation, he altered one word of his usual response to 'What do you do?' He used to say 'I sell life insurance.' This was the one that didn't work. He changed his response to 'I BUY life insurance' to which many people responded with 'You BUY life insurance, what do you mean?'

He could now continue with his planned response.

'I go to the market for my clients and buy for them the precise insurance that fits their needs. Would you like me to buy some for you?'

What a tremendous difference that one-word change made to his sales, his earnings and his life.

Three ways we could start a commercial conversation other than the various ideas I have already covered are:

- I've never met someone who . . .
- I was given your name by . . . because . . .
- Last time I was here I promised that I would . . .

The opening of any conversation is so important that it is well worth while spending time to create and practise the words we will use.


# Self Questioning

Before we move on to the enthralling subject of body language in the next chapter, I would like to share some ideas with you on self questioning and information regarding what has been called the 'Super-Conscious'.

Self questioning is a skill we all use. Every day we try to persuade ourselves to take (or to avoid taking) so many actions. However, conscious self questioning can have us pulling from our minds so much useful information that it is well worth while discussing it now.

There are a number of methods you can use:


## 1. The Earl Nightingale Method

This excellent idea was put forward by Earl Nightingale in his classic audio cassette programme, *Lead the Field*, which I had the pleasure to re-voice for the United Kingdom market. It works as follows:

Take a sheet of paper and write a focused question at the top. Force yourself to come up with twenty answers to that question. For example, you might want to know how you can earn more money in the next year. Write the question:

How can I double my income in the next twelve months? Then write down twenty answers. I know, from having used the idea for so many years now, that twenty can seem a vast amount; however, once your mind gets into the flow, you may find that you can write more than twenty.

The beauty of this is idea is in the way you ask yourself the questions. The question focuses your mind past the point of having made a decision. The question goes beyond 'Shall I double my income in the next twelve months?', it presumes that that decision has been made and becomes 'HOW can I double my income in the next twelve months?'

This idea, The Earl Nightingale Method, is in my opinion one of the best self management tools you can ever use.

## 2. The Yesterday's Road Principle

This idea uses the power of pain and pleasure, the two main reasons why humans take action, to force our minds to provide answers.

This is how to use the method:

Sit quietly, with a paper and pen, and imagine that you have a reached a point in life, in the future, where you would like to have accomplished something. This could be a social, commercial or any other goal. You imagine yourself at that point in the future, taking into account the fact that you HAVE NOT achieved whatever it was. You then write down at the top of the piece of paper:

'I would have achieved this goal if only I'd . . .'

Then you listen to your self dialogue and write down everything that comes to mind.

This is based on two ideas:

- Questions are always answered, even self questions.
- You do have the answers to whatever it is you want to accomplish.

You can also apply the Yesterday's Road Principle by using the power of pleasure. The above example used the power of the avoidance of pain.

Using pleasure you carry out the same idea; however, this time you imagine that you HAVE accomplished the goal. You write a question to yourself as follows:

'How did I accomplish this goal? I did so because I . . .'

Then allow your mind to tell you how to fill in those dots.

### 3. The Mirror Question

This third method makes use of the idea that we feel uncomfortable telling lies to ourselves. If you take a mirror, look in it and ask yourself questions, you force yourself to tell the absolute truth.

'Did you really give it your best shot today?' would be a great question at the end of a day.

## The Rosenthal Effect

Research in America has indicated that someone's anticipation of an outcome has an effect on that outcome. It seemed that the anticipation was transmitted in some way to those involved in the relevant event.

This is what happened. A researcher discovered that when he gave instructions to a research subject the researcher's view of the potential outcome seemed to have a marked effect on the results obtained. Various experiments were carried out with the instructions given in a variety of ways – by letter, by audio cassette or even via a third party, all to no avail; still the researcher's view of the potential outcome had an effect. This is why the **double blind** method of testing new medicines is used. Neither the doctors nor the test groups know if they are using the placebo or the new drug.

Now this book is not the place to expand on the whole of this idea; that would take many books just on this one subject. However, we can use the thought for ourselves. Many people have stated that in order to achieve a certain goal it is necessary to visualise it as though it had come true. We touched on this earlier. Perhaps therefore it would be worth while to experiment with the anticipation of a successful outcome to our important conversations. According to some, the Rosenthal Effect involves use of the super-conscious mind, the mind of which we are all a part. Try some experiments of your own and see what results you get.

Another way that we can use the power of our subconscious mind is to ask ourselves questions as our conversations proceed. According to Professor Albert Mehrabian (author of a famous study of this topic), there are three factors of communication – what we say, how we say it and how we use body language to say it – of which the third plays the greatest part.

If this is correct – and my own experience would certainly make me believe it to be so – we can gain greater insight into what is being said to us by self questioning.

You will no doubt have had conversations during which you felt, that what the other person was saying just wasn't quite right. You had a 'hunch' that the words being used weren't that person's words or could even have been lies.

I believe that this happens because we take in all the parts of communication with another human being, but our conscious mind concentrates only on the smallest part of communication, the WHAT, the content of the conversation. Our subconscious, however, soaks up ALL of the communication, HOW the what is said through the use of body language.

Sometimes, this greater part of the communication seeps back into our conscious mind and we have that 'hunch'.

In order to receive more hunches we simply need to question our subconscious mind to pull back to our conscious minds the information it has stored.

Questions such as:

- I wonder why she said that?
- Why do I feel like this about what was said?
- What is he really trying to say to me?

Now this is not to become insecure or paranoid in any way, it is to use the power of our retention of incoming data and the power of questions to access what we have retained.

This takes us smoothly into the subject of body language in the next chapter.

# 7    Body Language:
# The Unspoken Truth


Can you imagine having to wear a blindfold to all of your meetings with other people?

Wouldn't communication be difficult?

Without the *sound* of language we wouldn't know:

- When someone wanted to speak.
- When someone disagreed with what had been said.
- When someone was bored to tears with the meeting.
- When someone was excited about what he or she had heard.

. . . and thousands of other non-verbal signals and gestures.

Wouldn't life be simple if all our communications and conversations were with a dog! We would know instantly the effect our words were having. We would see the wagging tail in response to our request for a raise in pay. We would see the downcast eyes and slumped shoulders, we would see the sparkle in the eyes at the word 'walkies'. Communication would be so easy.

And yet communication *is* so simple. People wag their tails, cast down their eyes and get excited at the word 'walkies'. We just need to rediscover the skills we have pushed to the back of our minds. Dust those skills, polish them so that we can again see the *unspoken truth*!

We have all heard of people who say they couldn't

speak without their hands and, yes, hand signals are everywhere.

The hands are not, in the words of the schoolchild's old joke, to stop the arms from fraying at the ends. They are the most fascinating and versatile of the human extremities. They are capable of crafting things with minute precision; they are capable of feats of strength barely imaginable and a delicacy of touch that is truly outstanding. These extremities have a language all of their own.

Let us start our examination with a brief overview of what we are going to cover.

- A quiz on body language
- Lying
- How to use body language
- Body language to avoid
- Facial expressions
- Handshakes
- Seating Positions
- Dressing with intent

Professor Albert Mehrabian, the scientist most often quoted when the discussion turns to body language, stated that the percentages of importance of the three major factors in communication were these:

| | |
|---|---|
| What we say | 7% |
| How we say what we say | 38% |
| Body language | 55% |

I was surprised when I first heard these results. I thought that it could not be possible that only 7% could be attributed to the 'what' of communication. However over the years I have accepted that it is most certainly a minimum part of communication.

Looking at the above figures you will realise that 93% of communication relies on aspects other than the words we use.

This makes all of us who are interested in communicating our ideas more completely, more clearly and more precisely, become constantly aware of our own and others' body language signals.

There is, however, a warning to be expressed about Body Language: be careful to avoid analysing only one gesture in isolation. Body language is what it says, BODY language.

## A Quiz on Body Language

Even with that thought in mind here is a quiz on twenty basic and common body language gestures.

Look at the pictures and read the description of the actions that are taking place and decide what you think each gesture may mean.

1  You are sitting at your desk having a conversation with someone and he or she leans towards you.

2   You are sitting at your desk having a conversation with someone and he or she leans away from you.

3   You and I are having a conversation, we are sitting down and there is not a desk or table between us. We are facing directly towards each other. As you are speaking I cross or fold my arms.

4 Situation as 3. This time I cross my legs.

5 You are talking to someone and as you explain your ideas you put out both hands, palms up.

6    You are talking to me as in 3. This time, however, my legs are crossed and as you are speaking I uncross my legs.

7    You are sitting on a couch or sofa alongside someone. The other person crosses his or her legs towards you.

8   You witness this situation. A team member goes in to see the manager. While the team member is talking, the manager puts his or her elbows on the desk, putting the fingertips together to form a steeple.

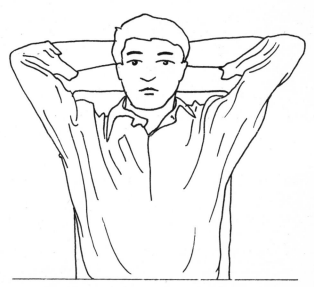

9   As 8. This time the manager leans back in his or her chair with hands clasped together, behind the head.

10    You and I are having a conversation. As I am speaking I put my hand over my mouth. There are two main meanings for this gesture.

11    As 10. However, this time the person listening puts his or her hand over the mouth. There are three main meanings for this gesture.

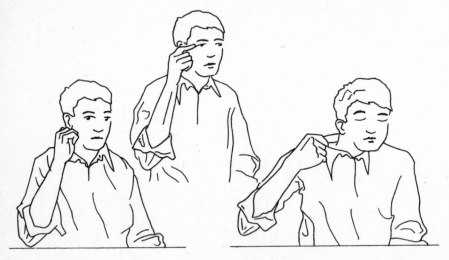

12    You are attending a seminar. The presenter uses some of these gestures:
  ● Ear pulling
  ● Eye pulling
  ● Collar pulling

13   You are watching two people who are having a conversation. As one is talking the other keeps looking down and away and is brushing imaginary bits off his or her clothes.

14   You observe a person in a meeting edge towards the front of his or her chair. Sitting with hands on knees, he or she seems about to stand up.

15    Someone has been asked a question and before replying he or she strokes the chin.

16    You see a presenter at a meeting hold the lapel of his or her jacket, fingers on the inside of the lapel, thumb on the outside pointing upwards. What is the significance of that pointing thumb?

17    An attendee at a meeting puts her chin on her fist and her head is starting to sag.

18    A saleswoman comes to see you. As she is describing the benefits of her product, she rubs her hands quickly together.

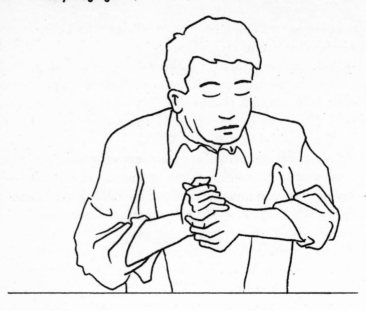

19    A salesman comes to see you. As he is describing the benefits of the service he is offering you, he rubs his hands slowly together in a 'washing hands' movement.

20    A presenter at a meeting stands with his or her hands behind the back.

I wonder what you thought about those twenty common body language gestures and signals?

Here are my thoughts on the meanings of those gestures. I must re-emphasise that we should never take a single gesture in isolation, even though that is precisely what we are doing with this test. This is to enable us to examine each gesture.

1    As a general rule when someone leans towards you they are comfortable in your company or interested in what you are saying. You can imagine that you are talking to someone and he or she leans towards you, eyes wide open in the high-interest position, saying 'Is that so?'

2    This is just the opposite. Someone leaning away from you may indicate that he or she is less than comfortable with what you have said. Of course it may be simply a change of position. However, leaning away with the inner canthus covered would be a clear indication of concern or disagreement.

3 and 4   Crossed legs and crossed arms can indicate that we are defensive or negative about the situation in which we find ourselves or about what we have just heard.

5    Palms up should indicate that the person using the gesture is being honest. However, this gesture is used in an exaggerated way when someone is being economical with the truth and trying to cover up his or her true intentions. In this use of the gesture, the shoulders tend to come upwards and the elbows are tucked further into the body and the person may glance away as he makes a so-called 'truthful' statement.

6    The uncrossing of the legs or uncrossing of the arms can indicate that the person using this gesture is starting to open up towards those with whom he or she is having the conversation.

7    When two people are side by side the crossing of the legs towards and away clearly says that they are comfortable or uncomfortable, interested or uninterested. Towards – positive; away – negative.

8    Putting the fingertips together to form a steeple is a gesture of superiority. The upward-pointing fingers show that person's opinion of his or her position in the relationship.

9    The hands behind the head is a strong superior or dominant gesture, particularly when accompanied by rocking in the chair. The person using this signal is exposing the whole of the body in a 'You can't hurt me' gesture. The posture can also indicate 'You can't fool me, I've heard this all before.'

10    The hand over the mouth of the talker shows that the person using this gesture is nervous about what he or she is saying or may even be lying. It is almost as if the individual is trying to hold the words back. Children are great users of this gesture when they are telling an untruth. They may even cover the whole of their faces as they say: 'Honestly, Dad, I didn't do it!' As we grow older we realise that the covering of the face is unacceptable and easily read, so we touch our lips or cover our mouths.

11    The hand over the mouth of the listener is one of the 'must spot' gestures. This has three particular meanings:
   ● That the person using the gesture thinks that the other person is lying.
   ● That the person using the gesture wants to speak.
   ● That the person using the gesture does not like what he or she is hearing or seeing.
   If someone uses this gesture when you are speaking, I suggest that you ask him or her a question such as 'How do you view this situation?', 'How does that sound to you?' or 'How do you feel about that?'
       The feedback from the questions will clearly let you know the other person's thoughts and which of the various meanings of the gesture that he or she has in mind.
       There is a strange thing that happens when you spot this gesture. If you say to someone using this signal 'You wanted to ask a question?', he or she invariably answers 'No' and then . . . proceeds to ask a question.

12    The gestures of ear pulling, eye pulling and collar pulling show nervousness or lying.

13    When the listener starts to look down and away and brush imaginary bits off his or her clothing, the suggestion is: 'I'm bored with this, I wish you would get to the point.'

14    As someone moves to the edge of the chair, apparently about

to stand, that is exactly what he or she would like to do. He or she is finished with the conversation and wishes to leave. This is another piece of body language that must be spotted. If you see someone using this gesture, I suggest that you finish the conversation or meeting as soon as possible or re-schedule. The person has stopped listening actively when using this gesture.

15 Chin stroking is a gesture of evaluation. The person using this signal is contemplating what to say next or is making a decision. Other similar gestures are polishing spectacles or pipe filling, all designed to gain thinking time. Watch the eye movements that accompany these evaluation gestures.

16 When the thumb is pointing upwards it is called a dominant thumb. A person holding suit his or her suit lapel with the thumb in this position is clearly saying that he or she is feeling confident and dominant. On occasions you will see a person with arms folded with thumbs pointing upwards. This posture or gesture can be considered as negative or defensive from the crossed arms and dominant from the position of the thumbs.

17 When a person supports the head with the hand, he or she is probably losing interest in what is happening. We can think of this as the person starting to fall asleep.

18 Hands being rubbed quickly together indicates enthusiasm. The gesture may also indicate that the speaker honestly believes that what he or she is saying will be of benefit to the listener.

19 Hands being rubbed slowly together indicates nervousness. The person using this signal may be unsure of the information he or she is giving out, or possibly deceitful.

20 The hands behind the back pose is a confident stance. The whole of the body is exposed to attack. Any gesture showing the body unprotected is saying 'You cannot hurt me, I feel confident.' The position of the hands behind the back can also be an indication as to the person's state of mind. If the hand moves up to hold the wrist of the other arm, this is a less confident position. If the hand behind the back holds the upper part of the other arm, this can indicate that the person is holding something back.

As I have stated on a number of occasions, and make no apology for repeating, body language is exactly that, *body* language. Take care to look at all of the gestures being used and blend your observations with what is being said and the way in which the words are said. In this way you receive the whole picture. Listen to your inner voice, your intuition regarding body language signals. Ask self questions to enable your subconscious mind to feed your conscious mind with the body language that has been subconsciously perceived.

Sometimes when people are first introduced to the idea of body language they have difficulty in believing that it is such a major part of communication. However, once we look actively, we realise that there is so much to be seen and learned.

It is an amazing fact that, with the exception of Jimmy Carter, every recent president of the United States has been the taller of the two main candidates. The taller candidate appears more powerful, more self assured, more in control.

In addition to the body language and signals we have discussed in this chapter there are hundreds of other signals and gestures that people use. One particular area of interest is the movement of the feet. See three people having a conversation together and watch the different foot movements taking place. The feet point towards the person in whom interest is being shown.


# Lying

Before we move on to how to use body language, let us now examine gestures associated with telling lies.

Whatever our activities it is a distinct advantage in communication to be able to spot when someone is being economical with the truth. Perhaps the greatest difficulty in this area is being able to differentiate between nervousness and lying. There are times when a person has been delegated to give out information and may disagree with that information. This will produce body language signals that are out of balance with the message. Despite that, there are a number of gestures or signals that can indicate that someone is telling an untruth. As with all observation in the area of body language, it is advisable to ask further questions to gain greater insight into the other person's true feelings.

### 1. Hand across the Mouth

We have already discussed the gesture of the hand across the mouth as an indication that the person is trying to hold in the words. It may be as slight as a quick brush of the fingers across the lips.

### 2. Restricted Movement

In some people you will observe a restriction of hand movements. Their hands will stop gesticulating when they are unsure of what they are saying. It is almost as if they are having to concentrate so hard on what they are saying in order to appear confident that their natural hand movements cease altogether. In normal conversation even hands in pockets have a movement. This is also restricted when nervousness is shown.

### 3. Lip Licking

If a person starts to lick their lips nervously this can indicate that they are feeling unsure about their words.

### 4. Nervous Cough

A nervous cough may be just that, a nervous cough. However if this coughing starts as the person starts to explain their position and is accompanied by other out of character gestures, we should be aware that they may be lying.

### 5. Blushing

Blushing is a clear signal that a person is uncomfortable in his or her surroundings. This may be as a result of what has been said or simply the presence of a certain person with whom he or she feels uncomfortable or unable to express true feelings. It may also be an indication that the individual is uncomfortable with his or her OWN conversation.

## 6. Erratic Breathing

Erratic breathing is a sure sign of discomfort. Only active watching and listening will enable you to be aware of the changes in another's breathing patterns.

I wonder if you can remember back at school when something went missing from the lockers or the cloakroom and the teacher gathered all the class together. The teacher wanted to know where the missing item was to be found and who was the culprit. Despite our innocence in the matter we no doubt exhibited all the signs of guilt. Blushing, nervousness, a change in breathing pattern, a dry mouth, lip licking and restricted movements. Everything pointed to the fact that we were guilty and yet we were innocent. Wasn't it terrible? And it was even worse if the teacher asked us a direct question. 'What do you know about it, Thomson?' resulted in a stammered 'Uh, nothing, sir.'

It is strange that there are so many signs of guilt in our body language even when we are innocent. The moral is clear. Sometimes sheer nervousness will have a person appearing guilty even though they are blameless. Be careful.

## 7. Foot Tapping

This is a signal often used by highly strung people. It may be an indication that a person wants to move the conversation along at a faster pace. It may also indicate lying.

## 8. Slight Fidgeting

Often when a person is telling a lie, the whole of the body seems to be under perfect control. There may be very small hand movements, hardly any facial movement, a clear strong voice and yet, despite all those signs of confidence and control, we see a slight fidgeting taking place. It is as if the person is squirming with the effort of controlling that movement.

### 9. Avoiding Eye Contact

Imagine this situation. You are conducting an interview. When you ask the interviewee the reasons for leaving the last job, he or she looks away while answering. This would tell all of us, instinctively, that the person was nervous about this topic, that there was something to be avoided in this discussion. We need to be aware of that gesture and be prepared with further questions to uncover the truth.

### 10. Eyes Shut

You will have seen, I am sure, people talking with their eyes shut. This would indicate that they do not wish to be in the situation in which they find themselves. They wish to be somewhere else. They are shutting out the uncomfortable scene. Try it for yourself. Close your eyes and say 'I am telling the truth.' It feels mismatched, doesn't it?

### 11. Flattening Tones

When people are lying there can be a flattening of the tones. For example, their conversation is usually animated in both tone and gesture and then suddenly those gestures and tones diminish. The voice takes on an altogether flatter tone. This may indicate lying. This is why active listening is such an essential skill in conversation.

## How to Use Body Language

We will now look at how we can use our own body language to add power to our messages and conversations.

## 1. The Face

If we wish to appear in control, perhaps in a leadership or management role, then there are a numbers of things of which we should be aware. Strong leaders do not go around with a large grin on their faces. In fact, less smiling will often be perceived as a more powerful personality. Now this does not mean that we have to frown to appear powerful or influential, simply that a more serious countenance will appear more powerful.

## 2. Posture

If you sit in a slumped position or stand with your weight on one leg then you will not appear at ease with your surroundings. Sitting upright with a straight back makes you look as if you are in command. Standing firmly on both feet gives an air of poised control and power. Head upright and eyes looking forward clearly show how influential you are. When you next have the opportunity, try standing in different positions to feel the difference in the message you are giving out and the difference in you that these postures create.

## 3. Steepled Hands

In our body language quiz, number 8 was the steepled hands and we are well aware that this is a dominant gesture. In a meeting if you wish to regain control, use this gesture accompanied by a deeper voice.

## 4. Dealing with Negative Gestures

How are we going to deal with someone who exhibits negative gestures or body language signals? Well, the first thing is to ascertain whether the gestures really are negative. It may well be that the so-called negative body language posture is one habitually used by the other person. We become aware by watching for the changes in position.

*Example:*
You are to have a meeting with your male boss and have gone into his office.

As soon as the boss sits, he crosses his legs and looks comfortable. He asks you open-ended questions and his eyes are clearly showing you, from the high upper eyelid level, that he is interested in what you are saying. In this situation you would not read the crossed legs as a defensive or negative gesture, simply as his normal way of sitting.

On a different occasion, the boss sits and does not cross his legs. As you begin to explain your new idea he leans back in his chair, crosses his legs and folds his arms. As you are close enough to be able to see, you notice that his lower eyelids have moved upwards and towards his nose, covering the inner canthus of each eye. In this situation you could certainly read these gestures as negative or defensive.

What do you do?

It really is very simple: ASK QUESTIONS.

- 'How do view what I've said so far?'
- 'How do you feel about what I've said so far?'
- 'Tell me, how does that sound to you so far?'

Three versions of the same question, phrased for the visual person, the kinaesthetic person and the auditory person.

This question should see a change in body language position. Of course the response may be a short 'Um, I'm not sure' with no change in body position.

What do you do? ASK ANOTHER QUESTION.

This position is clearly negative, so let us get those negatives out in the open so that they can be discussed.

'What do you see could be the problems that my idea might create?'

This might receive the reply: 'Well, now that you have asked, I don't think that it would work because . . .' At least now we have the negative in the open and can discuss the further possibilities or how you can overcome those negatives. So, part of your planning must be to prepare the questions that you will use to overcome or break any negative body language positions and gestures given out by others.

Questions such as:

'How do you see what I've said actually being put into practice?'

'What do you see as the problems associated with putting this idea into practice and how could we overcome those problems?'

'What's your opinion of what I've explained so far?'

'What do you think would be the benefits of the idea I've suggested?'

If you have a good relationship with the other person you could ask a question prefixed with your perception. 'I sense that you have some reservations about my idea, what are your thoughts?'

'It seems that you might not agree with me, is that true?'

'How could I improve this idea so that it would be acceptable to you?'

'How do you think that I could change my idea so that it would be acceptable to others?'

In Chapter 1 we discussed active listening. We know that if we can answer questions about what someone has been saying, we have been listening actively. By asking questions we are checking to see if the other person has been listening attentively and has been having thoughts about what we have been saying.

If the responses we obtain to our questions clearly indicate that the other person was not listening actively then maybe his or her negative postures and gestures were not in response to the content of our message. Perhaps he or she was responding to the way in which we delivered the message, in other words to our body language and tones.

When we ask a question and receive a response that shows that the other person was NOT listening, this must prompt us into changing our delivery or style.

### Over to You

When we ask questions that request feedback we can use a simple body language gesture to prompt the person to answer. Simply put out your right hand, palm up, about 6 inches (15 centimetres) in front of you and level with your navel as you ask the question. This 'over to you' body language gesture clearly indicates that we are handing the conversation over to the other person.

### 'Yes Tags'

We can break negativity by using 'Yes Tags'. A short series of questions which include the 'Yes Tag' will have the other person responding with a stream of Yes answers. This constant stream of the positive will see a change in his or her body position. This will give you the opportunity to ask more open-ended questions to uncover any negative thoughts.

*Example:*
Let us return to the idea of presenting an idea to our boss.

'This is a complete change from what we've done before, isn't it?'

'In fact, some people would have difficulty in accepting the idea, wouldn't they?'

'Perhaps some changes are necessary, aren't they?'

These questions would result in three quick Yes answers, which you would follow with one of the open questions to uncover the negative thoughts.

'How do you think I could change the idea to make it acceptable to others?'

### Something to Hold

When you are talking to someone and they move from an open to a closed body position, pass them something to hold or read.

*Example:*
'John, would you just take a look at this?', you say as you pass over a document or object.

For John to take the object he must unfold his arms. If he is leaning back with his legs crossed, he must lean forwards and uncross his legs in order to take whatever you have offered.

We must consider that communication is a mixture of mind, brain and body. If we are able to change one we will change the other two.

When one of those three areas moves the other two follow along. If we are able to change someone's posture by handing him or her something to hold or read, then for the moment that person's mind and brain will also change posture.

## Change Position

Yet another way to prompt change in another person's body position is to change your own position. Standing up and moving around while talking may have the other person change posture.

*Example*:

You are presenting your ideas to someone. He or she leans back with crossed arms and legs and appears negative. You stand up and move away while talking. This distancing of yourself from the other person may have him or her lean forward in order to pull you back into an acceptable distance for the conversation. The reverse strategy would be to stand up and move in towards the person. This is a much harder approach, however the individual's posture, which was defensive, may now feel too defensive at this short distance so that he or she may change posture. If the arms which are crossed become even more tightly crossed, move away. As you move away watch the difference that your distance has created and stop when you have the result you want.

You can experiment with different distances in a variety of situations to see the effect that distance has on the listener. As the listener you can change your body language as the talker changes position and you will able to hold him or her in the position where you give out positive responses. There is so much to body language and only experimentation will enable you to be more aware of the results that changes in posture and position can create.

So, to summarise dealing with negative postures:

- Ask questions.
- Involve the other person physically.
- Change distance.
- Change location for the conversation.

## 5. Evaluation Gestures

You have come to the end of the presentation of your idea and have asked the other person if they are prepared to go ahead.

For the moment that person says nothing and gives out what we can call an evaluation gesture.

- Chin stroking.
- A finger placed on the side of the face.
- Polishing of spectacles.
- Filling a pipe or lighting a cigarette.

Wait. Let the person finish his or her evaluation and make a decision.

The body language will clearly indicate what that decision is and then we will know how to react.

### (a) The Positive Decision

When the person has made a positive decision, he or she will move from the evaluation gesture into a positive position. This may be leaning forwards towards you. Other signs are high upper eyelid interest level, smiling or open body posture. It is obvious that the response is going to be 'Yes' or at the very least a positive question about your proposal or idea.

Wait for the Yes! Do not start speaking again until that Yes answer has been given or the positive question asked.

So many ideas are not taken up or accepted simply because the proposer did not have the patience to wait for the Yes.

### (b) The Negative Decision

When the person has made a negative decision he or she will move from the evaluation gesture into a negative posture.

The person leans away from you, perhaps crossing arms and legs with the face taking on a sterner look. What is the response going to be? There is a good chance that it will be NO!

This is one way that you may be able to deal with that potential negative answer. Do not wait for the No! We have covered the fact that the No answer will move the person's mind and brain into a negative or in this case more negative state. When someone makes a No decision it is as if he or she has dug a hole and climbed into it. It is then far harder to extract the person from that hole. Do not allow a No!

ASK A QUESTION before a negative answer has been given.

Remember the situation is that you have asked the person to go ahead with your idea. He or she assumed an evaluation gesture and was about to make a negative decision. You say: 'John, before you answer that, may I just summarise what I see as the major benefits of my idea? There is the fact that . . .'

You then go through the major benefits of your idea, watching closely to see the reaction that each benefit creates. Look at the eyelid levels, watch the body language changes. Leave a brief pause after the mention of each benefit. When you have discovered the major benefit that John, in our example, does like, repeat that benefit again and ask John if he will go ahead with your idea.

I have an important point to make at this stage. This idea or process is not designed to enable us to persuade other people to accept ideas and proposals that are not good for them, it is designed to enable you to present your ideas to others, in the best possible light and with a relevant benefit for the other person.

### (c) Dealing with Silence

Sometimes we ask another person if he or she wishes to go ahead with one of our ideas and the evaluation process takes place in silence.

This silence can seem to go on for an extremely long time. The silence can become quite painful. The pressure starts to build. It seems that the first to speak will be the loser in the discussion.

What do you do?

Well, there is a little technique which, if used smoothly, can work very well indeed.

Do this with a smile on your face.

First look left and right, as if to check that no one else is listening, then lean forwards towards the other person and say, in a conspiratorial tone of voice:

'My mother always told me that silence meant Yes. Is that what you mean?'

Remember that a genuine smile must accompany the words.

I used this idea in a consultancy role when I was negotiating an overdraft for a client company. It works!

### 6. Using the Hands

We looked earlier at using our right hand to pass over the conversation to another person. We need to be careful with the use of our hands, particularly with palm up and palm down gestures.

### (a) Palm Down

If you use palm down gestures with a pointing index finger, little or no eye contact and a hard-toned voice, this could be interpreted as dismissive at best or even insulting.

Imagine this situation. You and I are having lunch together and have had our first cup of coffee at the end of the meal. We want another cup of coffee. Seeing a waiter pass by, I point at him, palm down and with little or no eye contact say in a very firm voice 'More coffee please.'

That gives the impression of a very hard approach, with no thought for the waiter's feelings whatsoever. I treated him just as a servant.

I could have handled it differently.

### (b) Palm Up

Seeing the waiter pass by, I put out my hand, palm up. Looking him straight in the eyes with a smile, I say in a soft, pleasant tone 'More coffee, please?'

What a difference this would make.

In a management or leadership role we need to be aware of the difference between palm up and palm down gestures. You want to discuss last month's performance with a member of your staff.

You may not obtain the answers you are seeking if you stand above that person with your index finger pointed, your hand in a palm down gesture and with no eye contact say: 'Tell me about last month's performance.'

A better approach would be to have your hand palm up, with no pointing finger; having made eye contact, you could then ask softly: 'Joan, what happened during last month?' This would almost certainly result in obtaining the information you want; you would also be far more likely to obtain honest answers in a spirit of co-operation.

## 7. Matching and Pacing

If we match another person's body language in order to build rapport, this must NOT be 'monkey see, monkey do'. In other words, avoid matching too quickly. This will break rapport rather than build it. Simply wait a fraction of a second before you match another person's body movements or breathing. In this way you will create a bond between you.

Once the matching has been going on for a little while it is possible to begin to lead the body movements. The other person will be so in tune with you that when you move they will move with you. This is certainly influence at its highest level.

This can work well with anyone and works particularly well with young children. If a young child is upset you can using matching and pacing to calm them (though you need to be calm yourself). Holding the child to your chest, you begin by matching the breathing pattern – the sobbing of an upset child is usually accompanied by rapid breathing. As you slowly begin to breathe in a more regular and relaxed manner, the child will copy your breathing pattern. Slow your breathing down even more, breathing more deeply and more slowly, and the child will continue to follow you and calm down. If you accompany the body language with calming words in a deep, soothing voice you will speed the process.

As the father of four sons I have had years of practice with this technique and it is a major benefit for parents and children alike.

## Body Language to Avoid

Some of the body language gestures to avoid are:

- Pen clicking, which indicates impatience or nervousness.
- Barriers such as a desk or table.
- Fiddling with glasses or papers or anything else, which can indicate that you are bored or nervous.

## Facial Expressions

People's faces more often than not are expressive of what is happening in their minds. It is the changes of expression that you need to watch carefully. With the people with whom we deal on a regular basis at home and at work we tend to know what they look like in a variety of different circumstances or when they are making certain remarks or comments. But be aware of the changes on *other* people's faces so that you can build a mental file of how they look in different states. You will then be able to read their unspoken truth.

## Handshakes

A handshake is a rare opportunity to touch another person. Most young men are taught by their fathers to 'Shake like a man' and persuaded that their handshakes are a signature of some description, an indicator of strength and position. Yes, to an extent the handshake does have that effect, so take care not to miss the opportunities presented by the handshake.

Let me share details and use of the various handshakes with you.

## 1. The Parallel Handshake

The purpose of this handshake is to build subconscious rapport with another person. We do this by creating a parallel handshake. We match four areas of the other person's handshake:

- Speed
- Pressure
- Oscillation
- Time

By matching these four areas of another person's handshake we are in effect saying with the hand 'I am the same as you', 'I present no threat.'

This is how to do it:

When someone offers to shake your hand, wait a fraction of a second to feel the amount of pressure they are applying to your hand. Then match that pressure.

Maintain eye contact, do NOT look at the hands. Let the other person lead the handshake and match the amount of up and down movement (oscillation), the speed of the shake and the amount of time for which the contact is maintained. Release as soon as they release.

This will take practice but does have a remarkable effect.

There are two handshakes that should NOT be paralleled.

### (a) The Gorilla Grip

This is the type of handshake where the other person tries to squeeze the life out of your hand. Attempting to parallel this could end in broken bones. If you know someone who uses this grip, avoid shaking hands with that individual in future. Wave 'hello' instead of shaking hands. Have your hands in your pockets and simply ignore the outstretched hand as though you haven't seen it. He or she will eventually get the message.

### (b) The Wet Fish

This is the type of handshake where you feel as if you are shaking hands with a wet fish or bunch of limp bananas. Do not match this handshake; the other person will think that you are trying to be funny and rapport will be instantly broken.

With most people it is possible to match their handshake and with practice the handshake becomes an opportunity to say 'I am the same as you.'

## 2. The Questioning Handshake

The purpose of this grip is to ask questions with your hand without the other person realising that you are doing it.

These are the questions you will ask:

- How teachable is this person by me?
- How resistant is this person to me or my ideas?
- How flexible is this person?
- What is his or her strength of character?

These are all very good questions to be able to ask without saying a word.

**This is how to do it:**

You put out your hand with the palm slightly open. In other words with your palm turned very slightly to the right. This ensures that the other person takes your hand with their hand slightly palm down or with their hand slightly turned to their left.

As the handshake proceeds, you turn your hand slightly palm down towards your left, turning the other person's hand slightly palm up.

This turning movement measures the resistance in the other person's wrist.

I must re-emphasise that it is the slightest of movements and carried out only after the handshake has begun.

If the movement is too violent the other person will be well aware that you are turning his or her hand and you will instantly break rapport.

If the movement is done immediately the hands touch, this will also feel very uncomfortable for the other person.

This is what the resistance or lack of resistance tells you.

## (a) Resistance

If there is a great deal of resistance in the other person's wrist you can deduce that he or she is a strong character, at this stage possibly resistant to you and your ideas. You would certainly come straight to the point of your discussion and not waste time on too much small talk. You would use all of the rapport-building skills we have covered in this book to create a good feeling between you and the other person.

## (b) No Resistance

If there is little or no resistance to your turning movement, this indicates that the person has a degree of trust in you. He or she is teachable by you and feels comfortable with you. Be careful not to turn the hand too far.

As with all of the ideas we have discussed, it will take practice to master these handshakes. I suggest that you start with friends and colleagues who may forgive you if they realise that you are using a different handshake from normal.

The purpose of using these handshakes is to enable you to change your message to make it more acceptable to the other person's style of communication.

### 3. The Dominant Handshake

When someone comes at you with the dominant handshake, that is to say with the palm down, forcing you to put your hand in the palm up submissive gesture, you may decide that you do not want to shake hands in that way.

There are a number of ways to counter this type of hand-shake:

- You could attempt to turn the other person's hand over as the handshaking proceeds. This may not be a good idea as you may end up in a battle of strength and wills.
- Step forward to the other person, pulling his or her hand towards you as you do so. This will

automatically bring the hand back to an upright position.

- Place your left hand on top of the shaking hands, saying I am on top. This may result in the other person also putting his or her hand on top.

### 4. The Missed Grip

This is when you take hold of the other person's fingers instead of the whole hand. This can be an awkward situation, although it is easily rectified. Take hold of the other person's right wrist with your left hand. Maintain eye contact. Slide your hand into the full grip and keep shaking hands. If carried out smoothly with full eye contact, you will be able to rescue both of you from this difficult situation.

All of these ideas on handshaking focus our minds on how important an opportunity it is when we have the chance to touch another human being in this way.

## Seating Positions

Where we sit at meetings can have an impact on how our messages are received. It will also have an impact on how our views of others' messages are perceived.

As you can see from the diagram, the positions we will discuss are around an oblong table, rather like a board table, in an office with one door and one window. We will examine the various positions in relation to position Number 1.

**Position 1**   This is where the dominant person of the meeting is sitting.

We will call this the Boss Position.

**Position 2**   The Friendly Position

This is at an angle of 90° to the Boss Position and is therefore favourable for meetings with someone in that position.

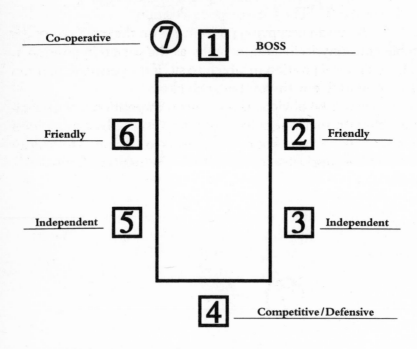

# Seating Positions

Co-operative ⑦ [1] BOSS

Friendly [6]     [2] Friendly

Independent [5]     [3] Independent

[4] Competitive/Defensive

**Position 3**   The Independent Position

A person occupying position 3 is indicating that they are taking an independent stance in the meeting. The distance from position 1 implies that they do not need to be close to the boss.

**Position 4**   The Competitive or Defensive Position

A person in this position has the whole of the table as a barrier.

This position can be competitive. I do not want to be near to you, or defensive, I need the protection of the barrier of the table.

**Position 5**  The Independent Position
   This is the same as position 3.
**Position 6**  The Friendly Position
   This is the same as position 2 and a good place in
   which to sit.
**Position 7**  The Co-operative Position
   A person occupying position 7 is on the same side of the
table both physically and mentally as the person in position 1.
This is an ideal position in which to sit, if the person in position
1 is comfortable with you being so close.
   It will be obvious if the person in position 1 is uncomfortable with someone being in position 7. The boss in position
1 will start to lean back as a means of distancing or lean
forwards aggressively, trying to push the person in position 7
away.

*Territory Testing*

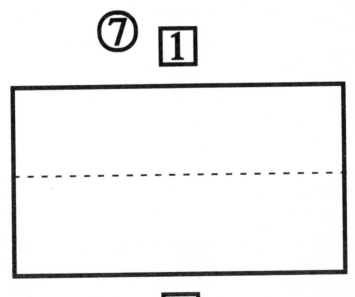

When there is a situation in which you can move into position 7, the co-operative position, it is advisable to do so. However, great care needs to be taken to ensure that you are not invading the territory of the person in position 1. This can be tested very easily.

**What to do:**
The dotted line drawn down the centre of the table in the diagram represents an imaginary line on the desk of the person in position 1. They are probably quite comfortable with you (in position 4) putting things into your section of the desk (A) but would possibly be uncomfortable if you put your things in their section (B). In order to test if the person in position 1 is prepared for you to move into position 7, the co-operative position, you would push a piece of paper or a document just over the half-way line.

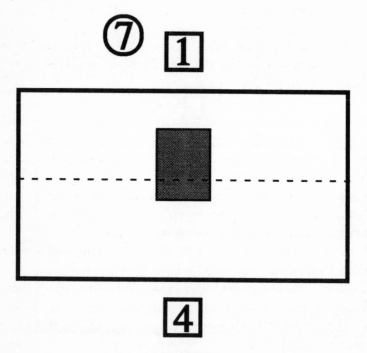

You would probably accompany this with questions such as:
    'Would you take a look at that?'
    'This is the report I prepared, would you take a look at it?'

'What's your feeling about point 3 on this report?' or any other questions that indicate that you want the other person to read something on the paper you have pushed across.

The boss in position 1 has a number of options, each of which would clearly tell you what you should do next.

- The paper is left where you placed it.
- The boss may lean forward and say something along the lines of 'Um, I see what you mean.'

This would indicate that you have not yet convinced the boss and you would be well advised to stay where you are.

- The paper is pushed back to your side.
- This time the boss may say in a more negative tone, 'Um. I see what you mean.'
- The paper is picked up and taken by the boss into his territory.
- This may be accompanied by a positive tone saying, with an interested facial expression, 'Um, I see what you mean.'

This is a clear indication that you have caught the person's interest and the taking of your paper into his or her territory indicates the boss's willingness to accept you into that territory.

In this situation you would slowly rise and move to position 7, saying something along the lines of 'This is the particular part I thought would be of interest to you', indicating the part of the document in question with a palm up gesture.

This move to position 7 must be done smoothly and slowly. A hurried movement will see the boss retreat.

You will be able to use the idea of territory testing in a variety of different situations. Experiment with moving items on any table or desk into the other person's space and see the effect those movements have.

There is an additional point to be made with documents. If the document you have asked someone to read is a lengthy one, I suggest that you leave the room while they read it. Silence can be difficult for some people to deal with and the silence created by their reading may be so awkward that they will only skim it. If you leave the room, however, you will give the other person time to read without the pressure of the silence. When you return, having estimated the amount of time that he or she will need to read the paper, and having stayed out of the room for that time, you will see from the document's position how you stand with that person. If the document is still in his or her territory you could move smoothly and slowly to position 7.

If the document has been returned to your side of the desk or table again, take your seat at position 4, knowing that you have more to do to persuade this person to your point of view.

The idea of territory testing is relevant to all human interactions. See the man put his glass down on a lady's side of a restaurant table. See the car salesperson leaning on a customer's trade-in vehicle. See someone sit on someone else's desk.

If we wish to check whether we are making an impact we need gently to invade the other person's perceived territory.

## Further Seating Positions

### (a) At a Round Table

With the boss in position 1, the person in position 4 is in a competitive or defensive position. The person in position 2 is in a *strong* friendly position and the person in position 3 is in a friendly position.

### (b) In a Restaurant

A great deal of business these days is conducted in restaurants and we need to be careful with the seating positions in those situations.

If you have taken a client or employee out to lunch then you would obviously want the atmosphere to be as conducive as possible to good conversation. There are three points to keep in mind.

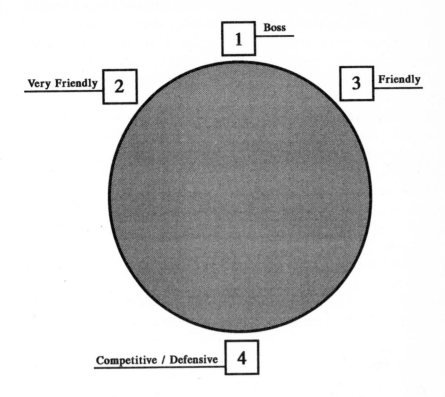

---

- **Back to the Wall**

Sit the other person with his or her back to a wall or partition. This prevents your guest from wondering what is happening at the rear. He or she will feel more secure.

- **Restricted Eye Line**

If possible, sit the other person so that the eye line is restricted. In this way your guest will not have a variety of possible distractions from your conversation.

- **Side by Side**

Again if possible, sit alongside the other person. This is exactly the same as being in position 7 in our previous examples.

The way in which you can best achieve all three of the above objectives is in a booth.

## Dressing with Intent

As a jury member may decide on the guilt or innocence of a defendant within a few seconds of that person's first appearance, so do we all judge when we meet a new person.

If this first impression is so important – and it is! – we must make sure that our first impressions are creating the right impact. We know that body language is 55% of communication and a person usually sees us before they hear us.

> *What you are speaks so loudly*
> *I can't hear what you are saying!*

**What to do:**
First, be aware of the impression that you create. Are the clothes you wear appropriate to each situation? Now this is not to say that we cannot be individuals. We can. However, many situations have certain standards or ways of dressing that are simply more suitable for the occasion.

I'm certain that you, like me, have been to parties or gatherings of some description where we felt under-dressed or over-dressed. It feels awkward, however confident we are!

So, for social occasions, if there is any doubt in your mind, it is advisable to dress up rather than be under-dressed. It is always easier to take off a jacket, tie or jewellery than to wish we had brought these items with us.

In commercial and business situations we need to dress with intent. For a formal meeting a dark suit with white shirt or blouse and a bright scarf or tie would be suitable.

The whole key is in the old expression:

> *To be well dressed is to be appropriately dressed*

## Summary

Body language really is the unspoken truth. As well as listening actively we need to be watching actively and this takes practice. One way to practise is to watch a video with the sound turned off and try to guess what is happening. Obviously this would not be an all-action film; a drama would be best. Then watch the video again with the sound turned on to find out if your thoughts regarding what was happening were correct.

Any situation where you can be an uninvolved third party to a conversation provides a marvellous opportunity to hone your body language reading skills. In a train, a restaurant or bar there are some excellent opportunities.

# 8    Open and Closed Questions

I keep six honest serving-men
  (They taught me all I knew);
Their names are **What** and **Why** and **When**
  And **How** and **Where** and **Who**

This famous verse by Rudyard Kipling gives us the six words that we can often use at the start of our questions to enable us to obtain more than just a single-word answer.

We are going to look at the difference between open and closed questions. This is not quite the same as opening and closing questions.

The difference is this:

An open question will usually, though not always, solicit large amounts of information. A closed question will solicit a small amount of information, perhaps even a one-word answer.

*Example:*
'Why do you think that it is important that man continues his exploration of space?' That is an open-ended question. If it is asked of the right person, the answer may have us sitting back and listening for half an hour or more.

'As the world becomes more crowded as each day passes, the continued exploration of space is a good idea, isn't it?' This is a closed-ended question and would usually receive the one-word answer, Yes.

'How many people work at your company?' That is a closed-ended question, obtaining the short answer '350.'

'Why do you have 350 people working at your company?' That is an open-ended question, the answer to which may well give you a great deal of useful information.

So, the closed-ended question receives minimum information, the open-ended question receives much more.

With closed-ended questions we receive three distinct styles of response:

- Agreement
- Contradiction
- Short Burst Information

For example:

'Do you like strawberries?'      Answer: 'Yes' (Agreement)
'Do you like strawberries?'      Answer: 'No' (Contradiction)
'What is your favourite fruit?'    Answer: 'Strawberries'
                                   (Short Burst)

We can use open and closed questions to control the conversation.

I like to think of these two types of question in this way.

Imagine that you are a fisherman and have gone to a river to do some fishing.

You have baited your hook (the *opening* question), cast out and the fish has taken the bait. Now although the other person is talking, you, the fisherman, are still in control. You are still holding the rod and reel and can control the movements of the fish by letting out more line or reeling in.

The open questions are in effect letting out more line. The closed questions are reeling in.

*Example:*
In a meeting:
'How interested would you be in decreasing our costs of production by up to 15%?' (the bait)

Answer: 'Very interested!' (the bait has been taken)

'Why have we used our current method of production over these last six years?' or 'What were the thoughts behind the introduction of our current method of production?' (open questions to let out lots of line)

Now, if the person answering the open question has swum too far down river, has moved off the subject or talked for too long, we need to reel in. This we do with a closed-ended question.

When the speaker pauses for breath – and even the most garrulous among us pause for breath occasionally – we ask a closed-ended question.

*Example:*
'When did the new system start?'
   'What colour is the main production unit?'
   'Do we own the equipment or lease it?'

An *opening* question to cast out the bait, an *open* question to let out more line and a *closed* question to reel in. A *closing* question, which we will cover in more detail later, would be landing the fish.

*Example:*
In an interview:
   'Knowing more about what you did at your last job position would help me to make a decision. Tell me what you did and how you did it' (the bait)
   'Will you tell me what else you did that made an impact on your previous company's results?' (letting out line)
   'How long did you do that for?' (reeling in)

As the questioner, the leader of the conversation, you are totally in control of the direction of the conversation.

Closed questions are easy to answer, as in 'Do we own the equipment?' 'For how long did you do that?' Maintain control. You are then in a position to ask another question, open or closed, as you decide.

For an important conversation or meeting we need to prepare the questions we will use. We need to decide if those questions are open or closed and give thought to the possible answers they will receive and what we will then do.

## How We Say What We Say

Some years ago I attended a British Telecom telephone sales course where the presenter used the word PICTURE as an acronym for the way in which we use our voices, as follows:

P   Pitch
I   Inflection
C   Courtesy
T   Tone
U   Understandability
R   Rate
E   Enunciation

### Pitch

The different pitches we use in our voices will change the meaning of our messages or words. We know that approximately 38% of our communication is contained in the HOW of what we say. The high-pitched voice can sound weak. On a telephone call it can sound irritating. The lower-pitched voice can sound more authoritative and can be particularly effective at meetings where we are trying to persuade others to our point of view.

Try reading this sentence in a high-pitched voice and then a lower-pitched voice:

'Shall we go ahead, then?'

### Inflection

If we talk in a monotone then we will make it difficult for our listeners to concentrate on what we are saying. Our audience will get bored and their minds will wander off into self dialogue or self talk. However, if we vary the inflection in our voices what we have to say sounds more interesting and will keep the listener's attention. Some have suggested that we end sentences by rising at the end. This can have an effect, although falling at the end of the sentence can produce a very strong impact.

## Courtesy

It is all too easy to forget to include everyday courtesy in our conversations. We are often the first to remind young children to say 'please' and 'thank you'. We should similarly remind ourselves to be courteous to everybody with whom we come into contact, be they family members or colleagues.

## Tone

The tone we use can emphasise the meaning of the words used. For example, say the following words using the tone that matches the word (i.e. a sincere tone for the word sincere):

- sincere
- pleasant
- happy
- sad
- confident
- believable

## Understandability

The understandability part of the acronym has a number of facets:

- We should avoid talking with anything other than our tongue and teeth in our mouths. Chewing-gum, cigarettes, pipes, food and drinks should be avoided if we wish our message to be clearly understood. Smokers should avoid smoking when using the telephone. The sound of smoke being exhaled can be annoying to some non-smokers.

- Understandability also relates to the jargon we use, however familiar it may be at our place of work or home.

Having been involved in the leasing industry for many years, I can remember a time when office conversations would have sounded to an outsider as if everyone had gone quite mad, or were using a language more fitting to an episode from *Star Trek*.

'How does it ref?, R & C, no CCJs, clear at both, True and fair, What's the profile, 6 and 30 with a 25% resid at 18 nominal!'

What a load of gobbledegook for an outsider to hear.

In fact the above means that there was a good banker's report, no adverse financial information recorded, the company's accounts were good and that the home addresses of the directors and the business address of the company also had no adverse financial information recorded against them. The lease was to be written over a three-year period with six months' payment on signing, followed by 30 monthly payments. 25% of the original cost was to be paid at the end of the lease and the interest rate was 18% nominal.

A longer though much clearer explanation for someone not involved in the leasing industry.

Jargon can be a double-edged sword. For those in the know, it is not only extremely useful verbal shorthand but can build rapport as the language is familiar to everyone. One of the techniques used by cult organisations is to have a language all of their own which binds the cult members together.

In public speaking using the language of the audience, its jargon and expressions, is a great way to build rapport and say 'I am the same as you, I understand your problems and opportunities.'

There are times, however, when jargon can have the opposite effect.

If we use jargon and the listener does *not* understand what we are saying, he or she may not wish to ask for an explanation for fear of appearing ignorant. This creates bad feeling; it breaks rapport. We need to be careful in our use of jargon.

## *Rate*

R stands for the rate or speed at which we speak. If we speak too quickly, our listeners may not be able to follow the content.

If we speak too slowly then people will try and finish our sentences or their minds will drift off the subject of the conversation or presentation.

It is the variety of speeds which gives power to our conversation. Slowing down to make a particular point, speeding up to add emphasis and excitement. This change in rate gives feeling and enthusiasm to what we have to say.

### *Enunciation*

We need to be careful how we enunciate what we say. We must speak clearly to avoid misunderstandings. Some people struggle more with numbers than with words, so take care to cite them clearly to avoid confusion. The letters T and D are often confused, as are P and B, S and F. Speaking clearly is the only way to speak if we wish to ensure that what we say is understood.

## Timing

The other area we must examine in how we speak is . . . timing.

A joke often becomes funnier the more it is told, usually because the timing of the joke teller improves. In our discussion of active listening in Chapter 1 we learned that we need to pause before we reply to questions to indicate that we are giving a considered response. That is the same thing, a question of timing. We improve our timing by practice. If you have an important meeting to attend or know that you are going to be involved in a meeting the outcome of which is important to you, I suggest that you write down some of the things you want to say. Then practise them so that you know the timing that will be most appropriate to those words and the emphasis you wish them to have.

In 1961 two psychologists undertook a study on vocal thrust
and discovered that there are eight emotions that play their part
in how we say what we say. Those emotions are:

- affection
- anger
- boredom
- cheerfulness
- impatience
- joy
- sadness
- satisfaction

Try saying 'I'm OK', using those eight different emotions.

We need to give careful consideration at all times to how we say
what we say, ensuring that we vary our usual style when
appropriate. After all how we say what we say is 38% of our
communication.

# 9     The Language Itself

In the last few chapters we have been discussing what is called paralanguage, that is the elements of language that are ancillary to language itself, such areas as modes of speech and the way in which communication can also be expressed in body language.

We are now going to move onto meta language, which is the language used to discuss language itself. We will cover the methods and words that are used to persuade and influence people to another person's ideas or points of view.

## Euphemisms

A euphemism is a mild or vague expression substituted for another expression which is thought to be too harsh or too direct. For example, when someone has died, some people prefer to say 'passed away' or 'passed over'.

Euphemisms abound within our language and can be very useful. They enable us to say what we want to say while not offending. However, when they are used inappropriately they can cause not only amusement but confusion.

In commerce the word investment is used instead of cost.

We have all been guilty of saying 'I'll only be a few minutes' when we may mean as long as ten minutes or even two hours!

We see brochures and advertisements that say that a product is NOT expensive, emphasis on the NOT, when in reality the

product may be an unnecessary luxury costing thousands of
pounds.

'I want to think about it' can mean that I do NOT want to
think about it. It can also mean NO! If someone says to you that
he or she wants to think about it, whatever *it* is, I suggest that
you ask further questions to find out exactly what it is that
needs thinking about. Often the excuse or objection 'I want to
think about it' is a euphemism for 'No', often the hardest word
for anyone to say.

'Send me a brochure' or 'Send me some details in writing' are
expressions that sales people have learned often means 'I'm not
interested.'

Estate and Real Estate agents have a language all of their
own, though recent legislation has attempted to clean up that
language.

| | |
|---|---|
| In a quiet area | Miles from anywhere |
| Lots of interest | No one has bought it |
| Compact | Small rooms |
| Perfect for DIY enthusiast | Lots of renovation needed |

Other words that are used to soften the possible bluntness of
our messages are:

**Only** Used extensively in front of the price of almost
any item.
*Only* $64,000, *Only* £2.60

Although often used it still softens the following price; perhaps
we should keep on using it.

**Just** Used to soften what follows.
*Just* carry this over there will you?
*Just* 5 easy payments!
*Just* sign here.

**Try** This is a strange word.
Imagine that you are standing behind a chair and
I ask you to *try* and pick up the chair. No doubt

you would pick up the chair. And yet that wasn't the instruction. The instruction was to 'try' and pick up the chair.

**Would I lie to you!**    Often a euphemism for 'I would lie to you.'

**Watch My Lips**    An expression that returned to haunt Ex-President Bush on so many occasions.

## Filler Words

Within our own language we need to remove the filler words. They may give us time to think, but they de-emphasise what we are trying to say. These phrases include:

- Um
- sort of
- type of
- well, you know
- you know what I mean.

Inappropriately used, they rob our speech of the power of persuasion.

## Link Words

There are times when people want to soften the impact of what they want to say and they start with a seemingly incidental and unimportant piece of information and then use a link word or expression before they say what they really mean. If you watch out for these, you will know how to focus on what someone is really trying to communicate.

*Examples include:*

- By the way
- But

- However
- Incidentally
- Oh and . . .

After these words comes the real information.

'You go home down the High Street, don't you?' Answer: 'Yes.'

'*By the way*, could you pick up my laundry while you are there?'

'I understand completely your point of view, *but* I think that we should do it my way.'

The word 'But' is a problem word in our language. It is like a switch in someone's mind. It makes them defensive because they know from that three-letter word that you are about to disagree with whatever they have said. Remove the word 'but' from your language and replace it with 'and'.

'I understand completely your point of view, *and* I think that we should do it my way.'

The word 'however' often comes before the real information.

'I'm sure that your idea for improving production is great, *however*, what you haven't considered is . . .'

'Incidentally' is another word used to link incidental and real information, as is the often used 'Oh and . . .'.

The easy information comes first and is linked by a casual 'Oh and' to the harder to accept information.

'The payments are *just* £100 per month, *oh and* of course there is the deposit of £200 to pay.'

The 'of course' used in the above sentence is used to imply that it was obvious to anyone that there would also be a deposit and that anyone who thought that there wouldn't be a deposit would be considered stupid.

All these words and phrases de-emphasise the unwelcome information that follows.

Words that can be used to emphasise the ideas that follow them include:

- Definitely
- Honestly
- Simply must

- Actually
- Frankly
- Literally

However, we need to think carefully about using these words. At times their use might imply that the information that follows is untrue.

*Examples:*
I *definitely* feel that we need to upgrade our home computer, Dad.'
   'Honestly, Mom, I didn't do it!'
   'I *simply must* start that exercise programme.'
   'Well, *actually*, now that you mention it, I hadn't thought of it before.'
   'Frankly, I just don't know what to say.' This sounds as if the person knows exactly what he or she wants to say and is avoiding saying it.
   The worst culprit of all is the word, 'Literally', which seems to indicate the opposite of its intended meaning.
   'Literally thousands of people have tried the new miracle carpet cleaner.' This may mean that only a few people have tried it and that the manufacturer would like thousands to try the new miracle carpet cleaner.
   So, with these words, take care with them in your own language and listen and watch out for them in others' messages.

## Vocal Emphasis

The vocal emphasis given to different words in a sentence can totally alter the meaning of the sentence. When you are to have important conversations it is advisable to practise where you will put the emphasis to ensure that your message is received in the way you intended.
   Read out the sentence 'Do you still beat your dog?' with the emphasis on the italicised word, as follows, and hear the difference in meaning that emphasis creates:

> ● Do *you* still beat your dog?

This means do you, as opposed to someone else, still beat your dog.

> ● Do you *still* beat your dog?

This means have you kept up the practice of beating your dog.

> ● Do you still *beat* your dog?

This means do you beat, as opposed to smack, stroke or feed, your dog.

> ● Do you still beat *your* dog?

This means do you still beat YOUR dog as opposed to anybody else's dog.

> ● Do you still beat your *dog*?

This means do you still beat your dog as opposed to your cat.

What a difference is made simply by changing the emphasis.

## The Words and Ways of Persuasion

I will start this section by sharing with you a simple card trick that amply demonstrates how we believe we are making our choice while being manipulated by others. You will be able to demonstrate this card trick most effectively with children. Adults soon realise what is happening; this does not affect the basic idea.

You and I are the two people involved.

The final answer will be **the Ace of Hearts**.

ME: Do you play cards?
YOU: Yes.

ME:    Would you just name the four suits in a pack of cards?
YOU:   Yes. Hearts, Clubs, Diamonds and Spades.
ME:    Thank you, would you now just name two of those?
YOU:   Hearts and Spades.
ME:    Hearts and Spades?
YOU:   Yes.
ME:    Will you now just name one of those two suits?
YOU:   Spades.
ME:    Spades?
YOU:   Yes.
ME:    OK, that leaves Hearts, doesn't it?
YOU:   Yes.
ME:    Will you remember Hearts?
YOU:   Yes.
ME:    Will you name the top four cards in a suit?
YOU:   Ace, King, Queen, Jack.
ME:    Ace, King, Queen and Jack?
YOU:   Yes.
ME:    Will you now just name two of those?
YOU:   Yes, King and Queen.
ME:    King and Queen?
YOU:   Yes.
ME:    That leaves Ace and Jack, doesn't it?
YOU:   Yes.
ME:    Will you now just name one of those two?
YOU:   Ace.
ME:    So, the card you picked was **the Ace of Hearts**.
       That's right, isn't it?
YOU:   YES.

You can clearly see what I have done. When you picked the suit
I wanted you to pick, I held it for the next choice. When you
picked the suit I didn't want, the phrase, 'So that leaves . . .',
made you pick whatever I wanted you to pick.

If you had picked Ace and Jack instead of King and Queen, I
would have said 'OK, name one of those two.' If you had said
'Jack', I would have said, 'And that leaves the Ace.'

This is simply a way of implementing the 'Yes Tag'.

Have fun with children you know.

Well, how does this relate to persuasion and influence? This is how we start to realise which questions we need to ask to persuade someone to our point of view. We start the conversation having decided what we want as the eventual outcome and then work backwards through a series of questions that would take someone to that point, by their own answers.

### Let me give you a commercial example:

I am in a sales role and you are a potential buyer. I want you to buy, let's say, a computer. The *investment* would be 5,000. It doesn't matter which currency we use for the example.

I want you to have the computer on a finance arrangement because I think that you are more likely to say 'Yes', and I earn a commission from the finance company for any business I pass on.

So, we have discussed the benefits of the computer system and I have asked you to buy. You ask how much it will cost.

I then move into my pre-planned maze of questions, in exactly the same way as forcing the Ace of Hearts.

I am going to take you down a road where you really have only one choice. That choice is to say 'Yes' to the computer system on finance.

In response to your question 'How much is it?', I say:

'I think that we have agreed that by having the computer system you will have at least two hours to use more productively each week, isn't that so?' You answer: 'Yes.'

I continue with: 'My accountant (solicitor, therapist or whatever profession you care to choose) tells me that he charges his time out at 50 per hour, how much is your time worth, 50, 60, 70 per hour?'

You respond: 'Well, if the accountant charges his time at 50 per hour I must be worth at least that much.'

My response: 'So two hours of your time is worth at least 100, isn't it?' 'Yes.' 'And you will have two hours to use more productively (pause) so, if your new computer system is an investment of less than 100 per week, you would be well pleased, wouldn't you?' Answer: 'Um, yes.'

'Well, it will be an investment of only 4 per day, 28 per week, that is well worth while, isn't it?' Answer: 'Yes.'

You can see what has happened, albeit I have used blunt questions to demonstrate the principle.

When we place an advertisement for staff we can use much the same idea. We work back from the description of the ideal candidate through a series of 'must haves' for the job on offer.

Before legislation prevented companies from specifying age, gender, colour, creed or other discrimination, job advertisements listed a maze of particular requirements.

To apply for this job you must:

Be between 25–35, be female, have Spanish as your first language, have a clean driving licence and live within 2 miles of our offices.

These 'must haves' now come in different forms and guises, all·designed to reach the pre-planned outcome.

So, if you are going to attempt to persuade someone to your view – a technique that involves a *thoughtful* process, work out the outcome you want and work back through the series of questions that will take the other person through a maze towards the outcome.

Let me again make the point about manipulation and motivation. If we use these ideas to persuade someone to our way, there is a fine line between manipulation and motivation.

If we have given thought to how to deliver our message in the most favourable light and with a win/win situation in mind, that is simply motivation.

If we use these ideas to persuade others to do things which are immediately or ultimately bad for them, that is manipulation.

Manipulation will only ever produce a short-term gain and long-term loss. It is bad in business, equally bad at home. It destroys rather than builds rapport and relationships.

## Psychological Needs

All of us are influenced and persuaded to take action in order to meet our psychological needs.

There are fourteen prime needs, two particularly important ones and twelve others.

1   Personal Power
    We all wish to have a feeling of personal power, whether this is buying something, to show we can afford it, or discussing something to show our knowledge of a subject.
2   Ego gratification, pride, importance
    We all like to feel proud of ourselves, our accomplishments or possessions. Our egos do need massaging from time to time. Everyone likes to hear honest praise.
3   Curiosity
4   Love, both loving and being loved
5   Emotional security
6   Belonging (to a group)
7   Recognition of efforts
8   Approval of our peer group
9   The chance to be creative
10  Freedom and privacy
11  Financial success (as we individually define it)
12  Self esteem
13  Self respect
14  Winning

These are for the most part self explanatory, hence need no discussion here.

Those who influence or persuade us are, in fact, making us realise that certain actions will have us satisfying one or more of our psychological needs.

All of these needs are met by drives and the drives are two-faced. One face is gain, the other is pain. I like to think of them like the old mask symbols for the theatre. We take every action, whether by the persuasion of others or ourselves, in order to avoid pain, or gain pleasure. When I say by the persuasion of others I mean that their words and actions were the catalyst for our internal motivation to take action to come into play. We cannot be motivated by someone else. We can only be self motivated.

Think about that for a moment, the only reason we do anything is to avoid pain or gain pleasure. It is true, isn't it?

Those who fully realise this and understand the psychological needs and the words to use are able to persuade others more easily. By focusing on the pain of inaction and the pleasure of action, specifically targeting the satisfaction of a realised psychological need.

If we listen to others speaking, as actively as possible, we will hear which of their needs their speech is centred upon, which need they are trying to satisfy. It is so simple to learn by active listening.

Let me suggest that you make a list of these psychological needs on a piece of card or in the back of your diary or day planner and when you have had a conversation with someone take a moment to look at the list. Then you can decide which of their psychological needs they were trying to satisfy by the main thrust of their conversation. After a few times of doing this, you will hear almost immediately which needs are in play. If you wish to build rapport with someone else, make sure that you are satisfying their needs while satisfying yours. A true win/win conversation.

## Automatic Response Mechanisms

We are influenced to do things, to take actions by certain automatic response mechanisms we have created in our minds.

We tend to comply with a request if someone uses the combination of words: Need and Because.

In 1978, the American social psychologist Ellen Langer and her colleagues Chanowitz and Blank undertook an experiment. They asked people in a queue waiting to use a photocopying machine if the researcher could take their copies first.

Naturally people were somewhat reluctant to let the researcher jump the queue. However, when the words 'I *need* to take five copies *because* I am in a rush' were used, 94% of people agreed with the request. It was also found that almost any words after the key word 'because' would work. Langer had definitely found a compliance trigger.

A number of tests have been undertaken with telephone salespeople in the UK. At the time of writing the results are not sufficiently conclusive to publish. They are indicating similar responses to the American experiment.

These automatic response mechanisms work for us and against us. As we grow up we use our memories to enable us to make *short-cut* decisions, rather than analyse every possible course of action we take throughout our daily lives. You can imagine if you stopped and made a conscious decision about everything you did. That would take an inordinate amount of time. That's why we take short-cut decisions. Unfortunately while we are often right to do so, these short-cut decisions can lead us into errors of judgement.

*Example:*
We tend to believe 'experts'. If an expert says it is right, it must be right, though perhaps not so. Who says that the person is an expert? What this short-cut decision does is to save us the bother of analysing the information we receive.

We tend to believe authority figures, people with titles of ANY description, the Chief Executive, the Chairperson, the Professor, the Sergeant, the Police Officer, the Manager.

We believe those who have uniforms of authority. Police officers, firemen, medical staff and even those who dress powerfully in a business or social setting.

We would be less likely to believe the lessons taught by the golf pro if he or she was wearing a business suit on the practice ground.

We also believe those who have the trappings of authority – the large car, the large desk, the large office, the large house – all short-cut automatic response mechanism decisions.

We need to take care because there are those who may take advantage of us by appearing to be experts, by appearing to be in a position of authority.

Children aren't taken in by these trappings. They have not yet learned the automatic responses so they keep asking 'Why?' Perhaps we all need to ask 'Why? Who says so?' more often.

On the reverse side of the coin we must clearly see that to

persuade others more easily we can use the automatic responses, dressing appropriately to the situation in which we wish to persuade.

## The Drop Sell

A technique or method called the Drop Sell is often used to influence our actions. Variously known as Hurt and Rescue, or Kill & Cure, this method involves someone in asking us to do something far in excess of what he or she really wants us to do, far in excess of what we might consider reasonable in the circumstances, then moving to a lower position of request to which we can agree more easily. We agree more easily because the second request is so far behind or has dropped so low from the first request.

*Example:*
Let us say that I want one of my sons to baby-sit for his younger brothers on Saturday night. I could say:
   'I need you to baby-sit for your younger brothers on the next seven Saturday nights, because your mother and I have a number of important functions to go to.'
   Response: 'Oh, Dad!'
   'Well, perhaps just every other Saturday night for the next few weeks.'
   Response: 'Dad, I've arranged to go out with my friends to the . . . (whatever is the in-place of the moment).
   'OK, I understand that, just this Saturday night then? It is really important that your mother and I are there.'
   Response: 'OK, Dad.'
   You realise that I wouldn't dream of using this ploy on my children, but it clearly illustrates the Drop Sell method.
   I remember watching a documentary television programme about a well-known comedian. He had started in radio and some of his jokes were to say the least somewhat risqué for those times. He developed a technique for getting those jokes and (for those days) offensive words through the radio censors.
   He would include something so rude that it was bound to be

refused and he would then compromise with the censors by agreeing to remove the offending words as long as everything else was left in.

That was a Drop Sell, Hurt and Rescue, Kill & Cure method. It doesn't matter what we call it, it still works and is used upon us by those who understand how and why people are persuaded to take action.

## The Differences in the Offers

The difference in two or more offers can influence our decisions. When we have agreed to buy a large item, we are more easily persuaded to buy a second smaller one. Try this experiment for yourself. Have three buckets or containers and put hot water into the first, cold water into the second and warm water into the third. Taking care that the hot water is not too hot, put one hand in the hot water and the other in the cold water. After about 30 seconds put BOTH hands in the warm water. You should feel with the hand that was in the hot water that the warm water feels cold. The hand that was in the cold water will feel that the warm water is hot! It is all about the difference. It is the difference that matters.

This relates to persuasion in this way. When we buy an expensive item – a car, a house or even someone's idea leading to a major decision, we will more easily buy a lesser priced item without negotiating the price.

*Example:*
You go to buy a car, it is going to cost thousands. After agreeing to buy it, you feel that the price of special wheels or a radio seem minor in comparison. And that is the key word, 'comparison'.

It would be exactly the same with a suit of clothes. The experienced salesperson will try to sell the tie or blouse or scarf to go with the suit *after* the decision to buy the suit has been made. The price of carpets and curtains for a house, when sold by the vendor of the house, after the house sale has been agreed, are usually not negotiated with the same forcefulness as the house price itself.

I'm certain that you can think of many situations in your private and business life where you could use this idea or where you have had this technique used on you.

Many of us will have had the experience of buying a pair of shoes and then being asked to buy laces or polish or protector or shoe trees. Unfortunately so many sales assistants ask us to buy such accessories with such a negative attitude and a thought pattern of no hope of success, that few of us do purchase. Just think if they understood how to do it, there wouldn't be a house in the civilised world without its own stock of laces and polish.

## Reciprocation and Obligation

We will now discuss some additional ways in which we are persuaded to take action or how we can persuade others to take action.

Reciprocation and obligation both have their part to play.

In many major airports and railway stations and even on the streets we have all seen members of religious sects giving away flowers. It must cost a fortune. No, it doesn't, and it can be a very profitable venture.

The technique used is one of reciprocation and obligation. As we live in a civilised world we are often under an obligation to reciprocate to others for favours they have given to us. So, the flower seller will 'give' you the flower and then ask for a donation. He or she has obligated you by giving you something, in this case the flower, and you may feel that you have to reciprocate by giving the donation. Usually those who take any flowers throw them away shortly afterwards and the flower seller's assistant simply collects them for 're-sale'.

A free sample works in the same way. We feel obligated to return the favour. Free samples are an extremely powerful way to sell a product; not only is it an honest way to let the customer try before buying, but it also has a degree of obligation built in.

The whole obligation method can see favours returned that are larger than the original gift and the method applies to the uninvited favour just as strongly.

This favour or obligation is part of the Drop Sell method we discussed earlier, in as much as the person asking for the large order or large agreement does the other party a favour by quickly moving from their extreme request position to a more reasonable request position without any argument or discussion. The person who has been asked feels pleased, or we could use the word obligated, that the person has so easily and quickly changed their request or expectations.

## The Free Sample

The free sample technique is used in many supermarkets and delicatessens, particularly with wine and cheese. We have all seen this in operation, for example the 'help yourself' basket of new cheese carefully placed just above the cheese display. Similarly, a marketing person may stand with a bottle of red and a bottle of white and a tray full of plastic beakers inviting us to try the latest New World wine. These ideas and methods are used because they work!

## The Puppy Dog

A persuasion technique called the Puppy Dog is also used to obligate us and influence our decisions.

The original idea came from Mom and Dad going to the local pet shop to talk about having a cute puppy for their children. The shopkeeper said to the children 'Take him home for the weekend and bring him back on Monday morning if he hasn't fitted in or if you don't like him any more.'

How could we resist that! Those first two days were bliss. There were no arguments about who was going to take the dog for a walk. There was laughter as he chewed Dad's new slippers, followed by understanding comments such as 'Well, he's only a puppy' as he howled all night long.

Monday is usually a work and school day and before we knew what had happened the dog was ours. Obligation, reciprocation, psychological needs all coming into play allied to good old-fashioned understanding of people and common sense. The shopkeeper in this example was also being extremely fair to his customers by allowing them to try before they made a final buying decision.

One well-known water filtration company uses the same approach. The salesperson will lend you a counter-top water filter, called a Puppy Dog by those who distribute these products, for a period of seven to ten days. Once you are used to filtered water you will not wish to return to drinking chlorine in your tea or coffee. It is the same idea, the same approach.

Similarly, some car dealers will lend potentially serious buyers a car for a whole weekend. This is done in the hope that by the time you have experienced the admiring stares of your neighbours and the comments of your family, the last thing you want to do is relinquish the car. Well, only if you can order your new model.

It is the same idea and it is a good idea, it lets the customers try before they buy.

The same process can happen with ideas.

You are at a meeting at work and want your colleagues to accept one of your ideas. One of the ways in which you may be able to persuade others to accept your idea is to propose that others try your idea for a week or a month.

It may be an operating procedure that you are convinced will make a difference or a situation at home where you are certain that a new way of doing things will lead to greater harmony in the family. The words you could use would be:

'Let's just try it for, say, one month and see what happens. At the end of the month we will meet again and look at the results and then make a long-term decision. That's fair, isn't it?'

This reasoned and reasonable approach will have many people agreeing at least to try your idea.

Influence and persuasion methods and techniques are used the world over, sometimes without the user realising what is happening. Conscious persuaders would include direct marketers, salespeople and advertisers. The professionals among those ranks test idea after idea until they find the one that produces the best results.

Wine waiters are a classic example. I've seen them in operation using such lines as: 'Might I suggest a particularly excellent wine, sir, it really is for those with a discerning palate. Yes, it is a little more expensive. However, I think you will like it. Would you like to try it?'

How could we refuse this obvious compliment to our good taste and mature palate? We can't and the price only enhances the offer as we fulfil our need for personal power by showing those around us that we can afford the little luxuries that life has to offer.

I remember one evening being in an Italian restaurant where the manager of the establishment said to a customer, after the customer had ordered a bottle of dry white wine, 'Excellent choice, sir. And which one would you like to go with the main course?'

I am certain that the customer had intended to order only one bottle of wine but there he was ordering a bottle of red to go with the main course. He had been *persuaded*.

When we are trying to persuade another person to our point of view it is the *process* that is often more important than the cost or price of their agreement to buy or buy into our ideas. This thought was superbly demonstrated during a seminar to which I had sent one of the managers of my company.

The presenter was discussing negotiation and had asked one of the seminar delegates to leave the room for a few moments. The presenter then called another delegate to the stage and explained that they were going to go through a role play on negotiation skills.

The presenter would play the part of a second-hand car salesman and the delegate would be a potential buyer. The presenter explained that the delegate had fallen in love with the car in question and had decided to buy it. He also explained that the golden rule of negotiation, in the presenter's view, was to frighten the other party with the first offer.

Sure enough, the role play started with the delegate taking the golden rule to heart and offering as his first bid just £2,000 for a car priced at £5,000. After some minutes of bartering back and forth, a sale was agreed at £4,420. The delegate returned to his seat and the presenter called out to him 'Are you happy?' 'Yes' was the instant response.

The presenter then called the delegate who had previously left the room back to the stage and explained, as he had before, the role play and the golden rule of frightening with the first offer.

The second delegate felt that he was a good negotiator and relished the idea of taking part in the negotiation role play.

His first offer, just like his colleague, was £2,000. 'I'll give you 2,000 for it.'

The presenter's reply: 'It's yours!'

Crestfallen, the second delegate returned to his seat. The presenter called out 'Are you happy?' 'No' was the reply, 'I've been done!'

And there is the rub. The first delegate had paid £4,420 and was happy. The second delegate had paid only £2,000 and was unhappy.

The moral is quite clear. It is not always the price of an item or idea we buy, it is often the process that makes us content with the outcome of the exchange.


## Giving Time

When we are persuading people to our view we need to give them time to make a decision. We need to give time to discuss the proposal, to argue certain points, to receive concessions, albeit perhaps hard-won concessions, so that at the end of the discussion they feel that they have played their part in the final details.

This is the same if we are dealing with members of our family, our work team, the other directors or manager, the sales team we lead. The time spent on the discussion is time well spent. Once people own the problem or opportunity, they are far more likely to own the solution. There is an amazing side benefit of this process. Once someone has agreed to an idea, be that buying an item or service or buying into an idea, he or she will more easily agree to further requests. It is as if once the door to agreement is open then it stays open.

We see this manifest with companies using the same supplier

for years and years, even though at times the suppliers may supply the wrong goods, may make mistakes with invoicing and generally not be as efficient as they might. The original decision and commitment to buy from the supplier in question still holds true.

This is also manifest with our children. It can take years to persuade them that helping to clear the dining-table is a good idea, is being part of the family. Once they *finally* accept the idea then they will help without even being asked. Once a 'decision' has been made a second decision is made more easily. It is worth repeating that:

> *Once a decision has been made*
> *a second decision is made more easily.*

## Positive Influences

There are certain types of people and situations that persuade us to say 'Yes' more easily.

### People

**(a) People with whom we meet on a regular basis in a positive environment**
If you offer social events and hospitality to your client, you provide opportunities to meet people on a regular basis in a positive environment.

**(b) People who praise us**
If we are going to use the idea of praising people in order to influence them, we must make certain that we give only honest praise. We must also be sure to praise the action and not the person. Praise of people can sound like flattery and is unacceptable to most of us.

*Example:*
When dealing with children we could say 'I love it when you tidy your room, thanks.' This is far stronger and less manipulative than 'I love YOU when you tidy your room.'

At work: 'Mary, that was a great report; it really helped me to get that agreement from the board, thanks.' Praising her work is far better than saying 'Mary, you are the greatest secretary I have ever had, I just don't know what I would do without you!'

## (c) People who are like us

We respond well to people whom we perceive to be the same as us. This is why taking the time to build rapport is so important. Take the time to establish common areas of interest, find out what it is about the other person with which we can associate and what there is about us with which he or she can associate. This is why dressing to the occasion is important; it lets others know that we are the same as them.

If we try to persuade a production team, dressed in overalls and covered in grease, while we stand there in our immaculate suit, white shirt or blouse, highly polished shoes and smart briefcase, it is likely to produce a dividing 'us and them' feeling. In order to persuade others we must find the areas of common interest so that they will feel that we are the same and that we pose no threat to them.

## (d) People we know and like

Think of the times in your life when you have said 'Yes' to someone and then afterwards retracted that assertion. In the selling profession this is called buyer's remorse. You regretted saying 'Yes'. Could it have been that you said 'Yes' because you knew and liked the person and found it difficult to say 'No'?

We all know people in our lives who will say 'Yes' to almost anything we ask. It may be your children, your partner or spouse, a person at work, your mother or father, a favourite customer or supplier. We also know that we need to be careful not to misuse the trust that those people have in us. Overusing that trust will finally bring the other person to a point where although they would like to say 'Yes', they have to say 'No'.

## (e) People's Appearance

We are influenced by people's appearance and will on occasions, rightly or wrongly, say 'Yes' to those whom we find attractive, male or female. The attractiveness makes us endow that person with trustworthiness, honesty, intelligence and many other attributes. From our own point of view we need to make the best of what we have. If we are to persuade others we need to dress to our best advantage.

## Situations

There are several situations that make us more easily say 'Yes'.

### (a) Scarcity
We have all been in situations where we have believed that a product will be in short supply. We have seen crowds of people rushing to shops to stock up on those items, creating the very shortage that was forecast. If we believe that a piece of information is a secret, in other words in short supply, we are even keener to know it.

### (b) A Sample
A sample of the product or part of an idea often makes us feel that we want more.

### (c) Limited Time
When we believe that we have a limited time in which to make a decision we will say 'Yes' more easily in the fear that the opportunity will pass us by.

### (d) Easy to Take Action
When in a commercial situation a company makes it easy for us to buy, we not only buy more but buy more often. The supermarket is the classic example of this idea. The super-market becomes a 'one-stop shop'. Shopping channels on television and home catalogues use the same principle by making it easy for the customer to make a decision.

### (e) Quantity Discount
We are prompted to make additional purchases when we believe that we will receive a discount on the price by buying more than

one item. If you are going to use this idea in your marketing, research indicates that it is far more powerful to say 'Buy one, get one FREE' than to say 'Two for the price of one'.

### (f) A Free Gift
A free gift with the purchase can prompt a buying decision. This may not be a free second item of the one we want, it may be something totally unconnected with the original item. I have seen coasters offered with books, calculators offered with photocopiers, free glasses with petrol, all persuasion items under the banner of a free gift.

We are all fully aware that these 'gifts' are not free, they are simply included in the price of the main item. However, someone would be less inclined to buy a book costing £12.50 and a coaster at £1.50 than they would a book costing £14.00 with a FREE coaster.

### (g) Speed of Action
Speed can also influence that Yes answer. Same-day delivery is used in business. The more impatient among us, having made a decision to buy, want the item NOW! Tomorrow is too late, we must have that new car today. The speed of action by the persuader can influence the decision.

### (h) The Way We Pay
Credit terms, leasing arrangements and finance deals all make it easier for customers to pay and therefore easier for them to say 'Yes' to the agreement to buy. £20 per month instead of £400 now can sound attractive.

### (i) Saying Yes just Once
Making an agreement once and then having a regular order or paying by banker's order can ease the pain of saying 'Yes' many times. Book clubs use this marketing method. Having once made an agreement for the customer to receive a book every month or every quarter, a regular Yes is easy to obtain.

### (j) Remove the Fear of Loss

This idea, which is also called Risk Reversal, is one of the most effective ways of making it easier for someone to make a decision. If we are able to remove all sense of risk from a decision, the other person will decide to act more easily. If you are in a business that supplies products, you may be able to offer those products to your customer and assume all the risk of the transaction by allowing delivery without payment. Payment only is made when the buyer is satisfied with his or her purchase. As I am involved in the audio cassette business, I know that this method of marketing is both fair to the customer and extremely effective for business.

## Meetings

In meetings we need to speak with confidence in order to persuade others at the meeting to accept what we have to say. We should not prefix any of our ideas with:

'This is probably not workable but . . .' or

'I realise that I am often mistaken but . . .'

We must speak with confidence, using all of the ideas we have covered so far in this book.

### Interruptions

Most of us will have attended meetings that have been interrupted for one reason or another. We need to have a method to deal with these unwelcome interruptions.

### This is how to do it:

If when you are speaking someone else starts to speak, simply put up your hand in the classic Indian HOW signal, palm towards the other person, and say in a deep voice, 'I hadn't finished what I was saying' and then immediately carry on making your point. This admittedly hard approach will stop most interrupters in their tracks and leave you in full control.

You will have made use of body language and the 'how' of what we say to make the method work effectively.

The HOW or STOP signal is used by police officers to stop traffic and is recognised the world over as Stop! The interrupter's response is almost automatic as he or she stops talking. Using the authoritative tones of the deeper voice, the square jaw look and direct eye contact, without blinking, will add to the effect.

So there we have a number of ways in which people and situations play their part as the message or carrier of the message. As with all ideas on communication, each of the ones we have covered in this chapter will need personalising, practice and testing to ensure your success with them.

# 10    Factors and Incentives

$Y$ou will recall that I quoted the famous verse by Rudyard Kipling about the six honest serving-men. Called what, why, when, how, where and who, they are useful at the start of open-ended questions. I now want to concentrate on the what and the why, both powerful words in persuading people to take the actions we want them to take.

## The What and Why

For the word 'what' I could as easily substitute other words regarding identity, for example factor, characteristic, the feature of an idea or item. The 'what' on its own is far less effective in persuasion than the 'what' allied to an *appropriate* 'why'. The 'why' of the 'what' changes in accordance with the person to whom we are talking.

Let me expand on this idea. I like to think of it as a train on a railway track. At the front is the engine, followed by the carriages, which are in turn followed by the guardsvan.

The engine is the what, the factor or feature. The carriages are the why or whys, the incentive or benefit. The guardsvan is the motivation to act, often phrased as a question.

The what could therefore be defined as the characteristic of a product, the component parts of your argument, the factor or facet of an item, the aspects, the traits, the make, the model, the nature of a person, the type of machine, the element, the module, the ingredients. Other words, the what could be regarded as the nuts and bolts of anything, tangible or intangible.

*Examples:*

- Someone is a good timekeeper
- A person has a positive attitude
- Someone is a good conversationalist
- A time-saving device
- This product is cheaper than a similar product
- The hotel we are considering staying at has a swimming pool
- The knowledge that others have accepted the idea we are proposing
- The view from a window of a house we are thinking of buying
- The make or model of a car
- A two-litre engine in a car
- The materials from which an item is made
- A company has been in business for a number of years
- The staff of a company are experts in their field

All of these are just factors, only features, only the 'what'.

These factors on their own will not motivate people to act unless and until they go through the thinking process of translating those factors into incentives to take action themselves. Alternatively, we do that thinking process for them.

Why is it that so many people in conversation only ever talk about the factors of a situation or item and leave it to the listener to go through the hard mental work of translation? A far more powerful and successful method is to state the factor and then clearly explain the incentive or benefit for the other person, the benefit they will receive if they take action or agree with our ideas.

The stated incentive must be relevant for the listener and not some generalised benefit applicable to everyone.

So the what clearly consist of the parts of an idea, item or product.

The why is how I will benefit from the what in action when I am the listener.

So these are the first two parts of the idea. The factor and the incentive, the what and the why. The incentive is the factor in action.

## Those incentives may be:

- The way in which profit I from this factor.
- The pleasure I obtain, specifically which pleasure.
- Recognition of how the factor helps me to avoid pain and which pains are avoided.

We know from the ideas we have discussed earlier that people only ever do things for their own reasons and that they are motivated to take action to avoid pain or gain pleasure. These are two aspects of the drives which come into play to satisfy psychological needs.

Some more of the pleasures could be:

- I have a greater choice in the decisions I have to make
- I have greater privileges
- I have leverage
- I feel good
- It is in my interest
- It makes a profit
- It saves money
- It saves time and therefore money
- I have a feeling of satisfaction
- I win
- I increase my worth or value

The third part of the analogy of the railway track returns us to the idea of the Subconscious Encoding Process discussed in Chapter 2. When we have stated a factor, we then continue by explaining the matching or relevant incentive or benefit.

We have to use the guardsvan as the motivation to take action or accept what we have said. We do this in question form. Let me give you a few more examples to make this crystal clear.

*Example:*
You are in a meeting, trying to persuade your colleagues to introduce your new idea for a system you have devised.

'We will need to move Mary and Tom to a different department (the Factor), which will reduce the costs of production enormously (the Incentive). John, how much do you think that will save us?' (the Question).

When John, in this example, answers the question 'How much will that save us?' he is starting to accept that the new system will, not might, be implemented.

You are in the sales business and you are seeing a new client about a new executive desk that he or she is thinking of purchasing.

'This desk is 7 feet long and 4 feet wide (the Factor). You will look very powerful behind this one (the Incentive). How many meetings a week do you have in this setting?' (the Question).

The question really asks 'How many times do you want to look powerful?'

You want one of your children to tidy the yard or the patio.

'The yard needs tidying (the Factor). When it is done you can have that barbecue you wanted (the Incentive). Who are you going to invite?' (the Question).

You want to make a decision with your partner about the best choice of restaurant for your anniversary dinner.

'The Casa Bianca has that singer you liked booked for the night of our anniversary (the Factor). I remember you really enjoyed his singing (the Incentive). What songs should I ask him to sing for us? (the Question).

Again I must make the point that these ideas can definitely be used to manipulate other people. You are aware of my view that if you use these methods to produce a win/win situation then you are using the ideas honestly.

This idea of Factor, Incentive and Question can work in many different ways. Paying someone a compliment, dealing with problems that you may experience with the people in your life, getting a raise in pay, used at an interview by both interviewer and interviewee. Let me share some of those ways with you now.

## Paying Compliments

So often when we try to pay someone a compliment the response is 'Oh, it's nothing' or 'It's really my husband you should be saying that to, he did it' or a variety of similar expressions unconsciously designed to push the compliment away. The inability to accept compliments is often created by low self esteem in the person being complimented. All we have to do when we are paid a compliment is to say a sincere 'Thank you', that is all.

So, when we want to compliment someone we should not only mention the factor, we must also say what the benefit is.

*Example:*
It would be easy to say to others:
'Great Car!' 'Nice dress!' 'New hairdo?' 'Great tan, Bill!' 'Good job, Brenda!' At this stage these are only factors. It would be far better to say:
'Great car, John, you look successful in that one.'
'Nice dress, Sally, you look very smart.'
'New hairdo, Sharon, you look great.'
'Great tan, Bill, you do look healthy.'
'Great job, Brenda, it has increased our profits and your chances of promotion.'
I know that you have the idea: the factor followed by the benefit as you perceive it from the other person's point of view.
If you know that the person to whom you are going to pay

the compliment usually deflects the compliment with 'Oh, it's nothing!', ask a question after you have stated the benefit. This will stop the habit of deflecting the compliment and enable the person to experience the feeling of receiving an honest compliment.

*Example*:
'Great car, John, you look successful in that one. Tell me, where did you get it?' When John answers the question 'Where did you get it?', he will have accepted the compliment 'You look successful in that one.'

'Great tan, Bill, you do look healthy, have you been on holiday?'

'Great job, Brenda, it has really increased our profits and your chances of promotion. Tell me, how long did it take to complete?'

So this is how simple it is to pay someone an honest compliment. State the compliment, the feature – great car, good tan, great job, nice dress – then state the benefit you perceive, then immediately ask a question.

## Dealing with Problems

### The NORA Method

When we have to deal with problems with people's actions at home or at work we can do so quite easily if we use the so-called NORA method.

Let me first explain the method and then I will give you a number of examples.

| | | |
|---|---|---|
| N | Now | The current situation |
| O | Outcome | The end result you want |
| R | Reason | A reason why the person should take the action you want them to take |
| A | Ask | Ask a question to obtain commitment |

*Example:*
Bill is a colleague at work who is part of your team. There are a number of occasions when you have to pass telephone calls to him but he has a habit of disappearing from his desk without telling you. This creates problems and embarrassing situations for you.
This is how you could tackle the problem.

| | |
|---|---|
| Now | Bill, when I have to put calls through to you and you're not there and I can't find you I feel embarrassed. |
| Outcome | If you let me know when you leave your phone I can take a message or deal with the situation. |
| Reason | We will then appear as an efficient team to our customers. |
| Ask | You could do that in future, couldn't you? ('Yes Tag') |

There are a couple of points that come out of this example and the examples that follow. We have not told Bill how HE should feel. We have told him how WE feel. We do not use YOU words, we use 'I' words. I feel embarrassed, I feel concerned.

The second point to consider is why Bill should take action. The benefit I have used in the above example is that 'We will then appear as an efficient team to our customers.' If Bill does not perceive this as a personal benefit, the idea will not be as effective as it might. The benefit must be relevant to the person; you want to take the required action.

*Example:*
Ben, your teenager son, is always coming in late, past the time you have set. You wish to correct the situation.

| | |
|---|---|
| Now | When you come in past the set time, I feel worried. I was concerned that something had happened to you, Ben. |
| Outcome | If when you know you might be late, will you just telephone and let me know? |
| Reason | Then I don't mind if you stay out later on |

          Friday and Saturday nights.
Ask    You could do that in future, couldn't you?

We have not told Ben how to feel, we have told him how we feel
as a result of his actions. This is far better than 'You don't care.
You are always late!'

    Then we have stated the outcome we require: simply a
telephone call to say that he is safe. This is certainly all I want
from my teenage boys, and parents I have spoken to agree.
Then we have stated a benefit. He can stay out later on Friday
and Saturday nights. A definite benefit for a teenager. Then
using a 'Yes Tag' we have asked for commitment.

*Example:*
You are responsible for placing orders with a supplier to your
company. Despite constant promises, the supplier lets you
down on delivery times again and again and you get the blame.
    This is one way to deal with the problem:
    The Set Up: Bill, I wonder if you would be able to help me?
    Remember that this will open up the Help file in Bill's mind
and will almost certainly produce the answer 'Yes, if I can.'

| | |
|---|---|
| Now | When supplies are delivered late I get the blame. |
| Outcome | If you are able to guarantee to me that supplies will arrive on time, |
| Reason | I will be able to continue to place orders with you and be able to tell my manager that things are working well between our companies. |
| Ask | Can you guarantee that this will happen? |

Another way of expressing this situation is:

| | |
|---|---|
| Situation | When deliveries are late I get the blame. |
| Outcome required | Guaranteed supply time. |
| Reason to act | Continued business and the manager knows that things are working well. |
| Ask a question | 'Can you guarantee that?' |

*Example:*
You attend a number of meetings and have some difficulties with one person who always interrupts what you have to say and finishes your sentences for you. You have tried the hand STOP without long-term success or feel that the STOP method would be inappropriate. In a quiet moment alone with that person you use the NORA method.

| | |
|---|---|
| Now | Fred, when we are in a meeting together and I am interrupted, I feel annoyed. |
| Outcome | If I am able to finish what I am saying, |
| Reason | we can both have our say, without interruptions. |
| Ask | Will you *just* hold back until I'm finished, in future meetings? |

We have used the word *just* to soften the hard request.

So, to correct someone's behaviour, state the current situation using 'I' language. State the outcome you want, give a reason or benefit why the person should take that action and ask him or her to do so.

You can also use this idea if you want a raise in pay. What needs or desires of your manager can you satisfy by him or her giving you the raise? Could it be a demonstration of personal power, pride, ego, self esteem or recognition of actions? What are the benefits that you would wish to tell your manager would accrue?

There are times when we can steer a conversation towards how the other person will benefit from complying with our requests. In other words, we could ask about his or her reasons for taking action.

'How do you see yourself benefiting from this idea?'

This is a very simple question to ask and will avoid your having to guess what the other person's reasons may be.

In a meeting you could ask:

'How would you see us all benefiting from this idea?'

'How would you benefit if we implemented that change?'

'How does that fit in with what you do now?'

If the other person states a benefit that simply is not available from your idea, you could follow with: 'If that wasn't possible, what other benefits can you see in this idea?'

The idea also works in reverse.

Let us say that someone is trying to persuade you to buy a certain product or buy into an idea. You could ask:

'How do you SEE my department benefiting from your idea?'

'Will you TELL me how we benefit from this?'

'What do you FEEL are the benefits for us in this?'

You will note that I have used the three main home bases of language.

One of your staff wants you to go to the upper management to ask for a raise on his or her behalf. The question you really want to ask is 'What does the company receive for this extra cost?'

This is better phrased as 'What shall I tell my boss are the advantages for the company of your increase in pay?'

Perhaps a self question before you go to your boss for a raise could be: 'What skills do I have and how do they benefit the company? What new skills do I have since my last appraisal and how will they benefit my manager or the company?'

We can use the incentive, benefit or why questions to focus someone's mind on why something he or she has suggested will not work. Instead of saying 'That won't work!' we could ask:

'How do you see us benefiting from that idea?'

'What are the costs of those benefits?'

'What are the downsides of your idea?'

All of these questions and their answers will let you know if the person has given serious and considered thought to the idea.

When you are asked to undertake a certain task or action you might ask 'What is the end benefit we are looking for with this?'

We can ask people to explain the facts or factors they give us by asking them to explain the incentive or benefit behind the fact.

*Example*:

In an appraisal meeting you ask someone why he or she joined your company. If the response is not related to the job itself (e.g. 'Better pay'), we can use any of the following ways to persuade them to expand on their answer:

- Silence.
- Simply say nothing at all, look at the person with an enquiring look on your face.
- 'And?'
  Simply say 'And' . . . and again look enquiringly at him or her.
- Ask: 'What has that meant for you?'
- Ask: 'And how is that better for you?'
- Say: 'Therefore . . .' in an enquiring tone of voice and then wait for the employee to continue.
- Repeat the initial response in a questioning tone: 'Better pay?'
- Say 'Oh really, tell me more.'
- 'How did it come about?'

The silence method is used by police officers and radio interviewers the world over. If a question receives a short answer, the response is nothing at all. The person being interviewed will probably feel more embarrassed by the silence than the interviewer and will start to speak again.

Remember to use the 'over to you' hand signal we covered in our discussion of body language. Put out the right hand, palm up, about 15 centimetres or so in front of you and level with your navel.

If there are a number of people together, perhaps at a meeting that you are leading, you can use this 'over to you' gesture when you ask someone to speak.

There is another way to let someone know that you want them to speak next.

*Example:*
Kevin is speaking and you want David to speak next.

As Kevin is coming to the end of what he wants to say – and you will know that from the words and tones that Kevin is using – before he finishes speaking, look away from Kevin and look directly at David, full in the eyes. David will know that you expect him to speak next and will have a few seconds, before Kevin finishes, to prepare himself. This idea also lets other people in the meeting know that you expect David rather than anyone else to speak next.

If we want other people to give us the benefit, incentive or why of each of the facts or factors they state, we can prompt this style of conversation by making sure that when we speak we do not only say the factors, we always add the incentives.

Before we move on to discuss five major types of person and how we should deal with them, let me finish this section by putting the ideas into a buying situation with a product.

- People do not buy logs . . . they buy warmth.
- People do not buy drill bits . . . they buy holes.
- People do not buy matches . . . they buy flames.
- People do not buy a garden shed . . . they buy a safe for their tools or a private sanctuary.

Nobody is influenced by money, they are influenced by what the money will buy for them.

When we are persuading others, we need to make sure that we clearly tell them the 'what' and then tell them how they will benefit from the what. In other words, explain *why* they should take the actions we have suggested or agree to what we have said.

## Different Types of Person and How to Deal with Them

Please pick one of the five shapes opposite as being a shape that represents you or to which you are particularly drawn:

The five different types of person are identified in some research by the shape that each type will choose.

The five types are:

Triangle    The Leader
Box         The Facts and Figures Person
Circle      The People Person
Oblong      The Person in a State of Change
Squiggle    The Creative Person

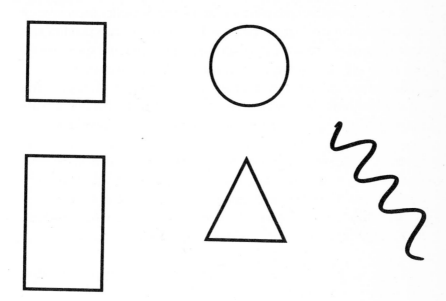

You can have some fun with this idea by drawing the five shapes on a piece of paper and then asking your friends and colleagues to pick one and see if they fit into the these descriptions.

### The Leader (Triangle)

This is the confident person. He or she will probably be quick-minded and focused in business. People in this category focus on the end result. They tend to speak quickly, make quick decisions, are risk takers and do not suffer fools gladly.

If we are having conversations with the Leader type we need to get to the point. Unless the leader instigates it, keep small talk to a minimum, right down to business. Give him or her two or three options only and ask for a decision. Leaders will not mind you asking. Be focused on what will be the end result for them. Focus on the goal we are moving towards and not the problem or situation from which we are moving away.

### The Facts and Figures Person (Box)

This person needs a great deal of data, lots of facts and figures in order to make a decision. Such people like logical argument and discussion. They tend not to be very good at maintaining eye contact and before they make a decision they will want to check out everything. The way to deal with the Box person is to focus on proven facts, proven solutions and a logical process. They want things to be smooth. They need the peace of mind to know that the decision they are making is definitely the right one and that there will be no comebacks. We need to lead them slowly forwards, agreeing one point at a time. The Box can be a person who procrastinates, putting things off, not wanting to make that decision just in case a vital piece of information has been missed.

### The People Person (Circle)

The people person wants everyone to be happy. Those who belong to this group are good communicators, emotional at times. They are team-orientated and will know the names and many details of their team members. They know their people well. We need to focus their minds on the benefits for everyone in their team, achieving happiness as a result of accepting our ideas. They are good listeners and make good managers. Sometimes they can be a problem for their managers, however, because they want every decision to make everyone happy.

### The Person in a State of Change (Oblong)

We do not come across a great many in this category. This person has something happening in their lives. Either they are thinking of a change at work, changing their job within the company or leaving, or circumstances at home have them contemplating changing lives.

The way to deal with them is to ask questions to try to uncover what may be underlying their thinking and, if possible, tailor your ideas to help them.

### The Creative Person (Squiggle)

People in this category tend to be excitable, even chaotic at times, very ideas-orientated and with a short attention span. If we have Squiggle people in our organisations or lives, whatever we do we must not try to turn them into Box people. It simply will not work. They can have difficulties working in a structured environment and if we have a lot of them in our company it may be as well to have a separate room in which they can all work together!

When we deal with this creative type we need to keep the conversation exciting and animated. Go for the broad brush ideas, do not try to fill in all the intricate details or they will just switch off. Do not give them too many facts at once and if they seem keen to go ahead, ask them to! They will probably say 'Yes'. They can be great to work with but they are a problem for the Box people who have to associate with them.

If you are in charge of a team or with your family, show them the shapes and find out their style. This will make it easier for you to tailor your presentations and persuasion to meet that style.

In one of my companies I had a board of directors comprising one of each shape. Board meetings were chaotic. However, I knew how to change my messages so as to have the maximum impact with each person.

# 11     Dealing with Objections

We now need to examine what we do and say when someone raises an objection to taking the actions we want them to take.

Some people have a style of responding and talking that makes it seem as if what they say is an objection when in reality it isn't, the imagined objection.

## Imagined Objections

There are five sources of possible imagined objections.

### 1. A Question Badly Phrased

Think of it in this way. You and I are off to a meeting with one other person. We wish to persuade that person to our point of view. Imagine that the person we are going to meet speaks only Italian and I speak only English. Fortunately you speak both Italian and English, so you are going to act as my interpreter. The conversations proceeds. Suddenly Toni, our Italian client, says, in Italian, 'I don't like blue' (I am only using this by way of example). I ask you 'What did he say?' and instead of translating his statement phrased objection of 'I don't like blue' into English for me you say, 'Toni asks what colours you do other than blue.'

You see what you have done for me. You have translated the

negative statement, the objection, into a positive question which I will find easy to answer.

Then perhaps Toni says 'Costa troppo', ('This is going to be too expensive'), a statement objection. I ask you 'What did he say?', and you translate the negative statement objection into a positive question: 'Toni asks if you can tell him so many exciting things about your idea that he will want to go ahead immediately.'

I would obviously deal with his so-called objections differently if those translations had taken place. When others raise objections to take the actions you want them to take in the form of statements, translate those statements into the questions that lie behind the statements.

In this case, the source of the imagined objection may be that it is a disguised question.

## 2. A request for further information

The objection may be someone's way of asking for further information. If they are not interested at all, why would they raise objections? They may need further information on which to base a positive decision.

## 3. It may mean NO!

So often people have difficulties in saying 'No'. 'No, I can't come', 'No, I don't agree', 'No, I don't want to do that.' People use all sorts of excuses instead of simply saying 'No'. For example, some people may say 'That's expensive', when they really mean, 'No, I don't want one.'

## 4. To check someone's belief in their idea

Some people raise objections to find out how strongly someone believes in the ideas they are putting forward and to test whether the necessary research has been carried out.

## 5. Genuine misgivings

There will be occasions when someone really does have genuine misgivings about what you have proposed. This may be that the explanation you have given is not compatible with their style or that you have given insufficient information at this stage. Further questioning should uncover the real problem.

There are times when someone will give a false or spurious objection. They may not want to give us the real reason why they will not agree. If we answer the false objection without knowing that it is false, we will be no nearer to reaching an agreement.

## Find the Real Objection

One way of finding the source of a real objection is isolation, which I discuss in full detail later in this chapter. The other way is to use the idea we covered before when we were discussing how to keep people talking when they have only responded with a short answer.

Imagine a situation in which you have asked someone to go ahead with an action. If he or she responds with 'I'm not sure that it will work', there would be little point in trying to defend your position at this time or trying to answer that objection because it has not yet been identified. You need to find out before you answer. Simply put out your right hand, palm up, as we discussed before, and say 'And . . .?' in an enquiring tone of voice. Usually the person will continue with the real objection.

*Example*:
'Well, I don't think that the staff would agree to a uniform in that colour.'

Bingo! We have the real objection and can answer it.

Whenever you know that the other person has not given you the real or complete objection, use silence, the enquiring hand or the enquiring 'and'. Do not use 'but'.

# Why Objections Are Raised

When people raise objections, one or more of the following three perceived problems may be in their minds.

## 1. Change

They are concerned about changing. They are resistant to the idea of changing the way in which they do things now or have done them in the past, whether in business or at home.

## 2. No Need

They perceive that they have no need to have whatever is under discussion, the item in question or the action we have requested. They perceive that they do not need the result.

## 3. Cost

The action you have asked them to take will involve them in expense and at the moment they cannot imagine justifying that expense. They cannot see that the benefits of your idea outweigh the cost.

Let us look at some examples of these three and translate them into the questions that are probably behind them.

## 1. The Problem of Changing

People will say such things as:
    'I don't see why we have to change . . .'
    'If it ain't broke don't fix it.'
    'We've done it this way for years.'
    'But he's always been on my team.'
    'But I always buy from . . .'

The questions that are being asked are:

'Please can you show me a way to use that idea?'
'What are the benefits of this change for me?'
'How does this help me do what I do better than before?'
'What incentive is there for ME?'

One of the ways to deal with this situation is as follows:

We ask a question about the length of time the current practice or process has been in force. 'When did you change last time?' or 'How long have you been doing it in this way?' Then we ask 'Why did you change last time?' or 'What prompted you to start doing it in this way?'

Then we could continue 'After all this time it must be worth looking at other ways that would . . . (here you would include benefits of your new idea that coincide with the reasons for change last time), isn't it?' or 'How would you benefit if you changed to the new idea?'

## 2. No Apparent Need

The objections for no apparent need are phrased as:
'The old one works well!'
'We've always got along with this one!'
'But you always stay in on Monday nights!'
'The system works OK.'
'I'm happy with my old one.'

The questions behind those statements are:
'How will I benefit?'
'What are the advantages of the new one?'

## 3. The Costs Involved

The expressions used are:
'That's expensive!'
'This will cost a fortune!'
'How much?'

All of these are really questions asking 'how will I benefit? What's in it for me?'

When someone says that something is expensive they may not mean that at all, they mean one of the following:

You've surprised me.

I didn't think it was going to be that much.

I have a price for a similar object from another supplier.

We need to ensure that apples are being compared with apples.

We have cash-flow problems.

It's outside my authority limit.

Asking questions and using the enquiring hand will soon establish what someone really means when saying 'That's expensive!'

I'm certain that when pocket calculators first arrived on the market, when facsimile machines were first available, when computers were first on sale, we all thought that they were expensive, that we didn't have a need and that changing from our old systems would present major problems. And yet, here we all are using calculators, faxes and computers.

## When to Deal with Objections

There are four main times when to deal with objections.

### 1. Never

Now I know that this seems a strange thing to suggest. However, there are times when I feel that some objections can be safely ignored. For example, during a presentation of your ideas someone might say 'It sounds as if it might be complicated to implement that idea.' Your response may just be a knowing smile and you keep on talking without direct reference to the objection.

In a selling meeting someone might say 'That sounds expensive.' You could simply say 'Yes' and then proceed to explain your ideas and how the benefits massively outweigh the investment involved.

Obviously we need to be careful if we are going to ignore objections. If they are really a problem for the person raising them, he or she will remember them until you finish what you are saying and then raise the objection again, having hardly listened to anything you have said.

## 2. Some time after the objection has been raised

We would do this by saying:

'That's a good point, Barry, I'll come to that in just a moment' or

'I've planned to cover that under my section on the invest-ment involved. I'll leave it until then, shall I?'

Again, care must be taken to watch Barry, in this example, to be certain from his body language and expression that he has let go of the objection for the time being, on the understanding that you will cover it later. Make sure that he has not been left with the impression that you said you will cover it later just in the hope that everyone will forget about that point.

## 3. Immediately

Often it is best to handle objections at once, even though this may break the flow of your ideas or presentation. You could say:

'That's a good point and I'm glad you raised it. Let's look at the implications now.'

'You said, John, that the idea might be difficult to implement. Would you *just* expand on that I idea so that I fully understand what you mean?'

The answer to this question will give you better clues as to what John sees as the heart of the problem from his point of view. When he has explained, you would say:

'So, if I understand you correctly . . .' and you go on to rephrase the issues to which he objected in a more positive way.

If objection concerns price, I believe that we should always emphasise that money well spent to produce a benefit or profit is an investment, whereas money spent which does not produce a benefit or profit is a cost. All companies and individuals invest in themselves in the hope of making a profit from those investments. The profit for a company may be in monetary terms. The profit for an individual may be the feelings they experience as a result of spending the money earned.

## 4. Before the Objection is Raised

This is perhaps the most powerful way to deal with potential objections and has a number of good side effects. The first one is that you demonstrate that you have properly planned for your meeting. You must have given thought to what others might say about your ideas. The second one is that you are able to handle any objection at your own timing, blending it into your presentation or conversation as you see fit. The third side effect is that you can handle the objection in your own phraseology and not in response to someone else's phrasing. Fourth, that you are obviously unconcerned about the objection or you would not have brought-it up.

You would phrase it like this:

'Now some people would say that this idea might be difficult to implement and they would have a good point, however . . .' and you would then go on to explain how easy the idea would be to implement.

'Some people would think that this might be expensive. However, I have carefully examined all the costs involved and it breaks down to only £100 per month. This is not a bad investment to yield £2,000 per month, wouldn't you agree?'

Handling objections before they are raised is the most effective approach. I suggest that before any meeting or conversation of consequence you think carefully about the potential objections that may be raised and work out how and when you will deal with them. If at all possible, work out how you will incorporate them into your conversation even before they are mentioned.

## How to Deal with Objections

Here are a number of ways in which you will be able to deal with objections.

## 1. Isolate the objection

This is done by saying:

'Is that the only reason that is preventing you from going ahead?'

If the answer is 'Yes', continue with:

'If I am able to share some information with you that would satisfy you on that point, would you go ahead?'

The only possible answer to this second question is 'Yes' because you have isolated the objection and then asked a conditional question starting with the word 'If'.

The idea of isolating objections works very well with the 'Box' people who forever want to go back over ideas you have already discussed. Therefore, if there is a main sticking point when you are in a persuasion conversation, isolate the objection by asking 'Is that the only reason?' and then answer the objection by clearly explaining why the objection is not relevant to your ideas. If the objection is relevant, explain how the benefits or incentives involved outweigh the objection.

## 2. Agree with the Objection

It is often a good idea to agree with the objection because from the other person's point of view the objection or their reason to object is valid. It is based on their experiences. Your view is equally valid because it is based on your experiences. You can use the following lines:

'I understand that your experience tells you that . . .'

'My experience tells me . . .'

'As we both realise those points, what do you suggest as the way forward?'

This shows the other person that you are not disagreeing with his or her views. Quite the opposite is the case; you are prepared to accept that we all have different views based on our judgement and experience. You are stating both views, yours and theirs, and asking the other person's opinion about the way to proceed. Make sure that you do not link the two views with the word 'but'. Link them with the word 'and'.

### 3. 'Just Suppose' and 'If Ever'

These are similar ways to deal with objections.

Let us say that someone is objecting to your idea of changing the way in which your company operates. The basis of their objection is 'We've always done it this way. Why should we change?'

You could use: 'Just suppose that you were to agree with the idea, what would make you do it?' This disarming method should reveal the real reason behind the person's objection.

If you are greeted with such a response as: 'Well, I'd be happy to try that as long as the trial was only for a few weeks', that may be the best result you can obtain at that time. You have to decide whether to agree or not.

'If ever' is a similar approach. 'If ever you were to agree to take this action/agree with my idea, what would make you do it?'

I have found over many years that the 'If ever' approach often results in a rambling response, the other person not disclosing what it is that would make him or her agree. If this happens, repeat the question, preceded by an affirmation of some sort: 'Yes, I understand that and, if ever you were to agree what would make you do it?'

## The 'Think it Over' Objection

Very often the words 'I want to think it over' do not mean what they appear to mean.

Sometimes these words mean 'No'. However the person saying them does not want to offend you, so they use a delaying tactic.

They might mean 'I am busy. Will you leave it with me?'

Most of us have been in this situation. We have made a recommendation to someone who responds by saying that he or she wants to think it over. We agreed and said that we would call in a few weeks for the decision. I am also certain that we did not believe that the person was going to spend the next few weeks thinking about our idea. In reality the next time he or she thought about it was probably when we called them for a decision.

We need to be sure that the 'think it over' isn't an excuse to end the conversation. If it is a real statement, we must clarify which parts of our proposal or idea are to be thought about so that the other person's mind is clearly focused on taking action.

*Example:*
You are having a meeting with a customer called Bill. You have made a proposal and Bill has responded to your call for action with 'I'll have to think it over.'

One way that we could start to find out what is really happening in his mind is this. If you have built good rapport or have a good relationship with him you could say: 'Bill, sometimes when people say that they want to think things over, they really mean that they are not interested. Is that what you mean?' You realise that to use this approach you must have a good relationship with the other person.

If you do have that good relationship he or she will probably respond with 'Oh no, if I wasn't interested I would tell you.'

There will be odd occasions when Bill, in this example, says: 'Well, to be honest, I don't see how this could work for us.' At least you would then know where you stand and could find out with questions what the real objection might be.

If we are receiving the response 'Oh no, I'd tell you', we need to find out what Bill wants to think over. This is how to ask:

'OK, Bill, it is a good idea to think things over. Tell me which particular part was it you wanted to think about. Was it the . . .?' You then go through the factors of your proposal or idea, trying to identify the problem in Bill's mind.

'Was it the fact that we will have to move John and Mary to another department?'

'Oh no, I was happy with that.'

'Was it the fact that we will have to make three people redundant?'

'No, while I do not relish that idea, I do realise that it is in the long-term interest of the company.'

'Was it the fact that the idea will take £5,000 to implement?'

'Well, now that you come to mention it . . .'

We have found the real objection, the price. We can deal with that price objection by explaining the value of the benefits compared with the costs.

This can be done by breaking down the costs to the weekly, daily or even hourly cost and comparing it with the benefits.

*Example:*

'The idea you are proposing will cost £5,000. However, once implemented, there will be no further costs for, say, five years. Therefore the real cost is £1,000 per year or £20 per week. If the benefits are worth more than £20 per week, then maybe we should be going ahead.'

Another way to deal with the 'think it over' objection is to say: 'It is a good idea to think things over. I have to go to another meeting now. Shall I come back at, say, 3 o'clock this afternoon for your decision?'

A positive response to this question lets you know that the other person is going to give thought to what you have said and you have set an agreed deadline for the decision.

If the response is 'Oh no!', it will usually be followed by useful information such as:

'Oh no, I have to get Brenda to agree to this as well' or 'Oh no, that is a board decision.'

At least you know where you stand.

If you are in a leadership role and dealing with a team member who is objecting to the tasks to be carried out by lack of action, it is a good idea to focus on the details and not on the generalities. For example: 'I want you to speak to 30 customers per day' not 'I want you to speak to more customers.'

## Summary

Translate the objection statement into a question.

Ask questions to ensure your translation is correct.

Use 'And?' with the enquiring hand to persuade others to expand on what they are saying and uncover the real objection.

Prepare before meetings and important conversations for the objections that are likely to be raised and how you will deal with them.

If we are well prepared, we can welcome so-called objections as others showing interest in what we have to say.

We can be like bamboo which can bend before the strongest storm and then return to its original position.

# 12  Getting the Yes

In this chapter we will cover one of the most important aspects of conversation, influence and persuasion. It is one of the most important aspects of getting people to agree to our ideas and proposals. In the sales business this would be called closing the sale. We can use the expression 'Getting the Yes'.

I heard a story many years ago about a man who had toothache and phoned a friend who was a dentist. The dentist was unable to help straight away as he was going away for the weekend and suggested that the man appear at his surgery bright and early on Monday morning.

The man duly arrived early on Monday morning and sat in the dentist's chair.

'Open wide,' said the dentist. On looking inside his friend's mouth, he said

'I'm afraid it will have to come out.'

The man was unhappy about this as he hated going to the dentist.

'Will it hurt much?' he asked.

'Not too much,' replied the dentist. (Mind you they always say that, don't they?)

'How long will it take?'

'Only one minute.'

'How much will it cost?'

'About £50,' said the dentist.

'£50! For one minute's work!' exclaimed the man.

The dentist responded, 'I can take as long as you like!'

It is true that sometimes it is easier to pull that agreement smoothly, painlessly and quickly than to hang on tugging and tugging until that reluctant tooth or 'Yes' is finally extracted.

There are four main reasons why people do not ask for that yes.

Yes, go ahead with the idea.

Yes, I'll tidy my room.

Yes, you can have a half day on Thursday.

Yes, you can have that raise.

Yes, I will order.

All the Yes responses we want and yet some people simply will not ask. Why not?

## Reluctance to Ask

### 1. Fear of Rejection

Some people are scared of rejection, concerned that the other person will refuse the request and that the No will cause pain. Fear of failure or fear of success may also come into play. Large companies have taught many people fear of rejection by making it difficult to get to the people who can say Yes.

### 2. Lack of Appropriate Vocabulary

If we do not know the appropriate words to use to ask for that agreement, we do not know how to ask.

### 3. Insufficient Practice

Once the words to obtain an agreement have been learned, practice must be undertaken so that those words can be delivered as smoothly as possible.

### 4. Lack of Belief

If we have no belief in the product or idea that we are attempting to persuade someone to accept, we will feel awkward about asking for the agreement. Occasionally we may have been chosen to do the asking but we don't agree with what we have been asked to ask. I'm sure we have all heard 'You ring them', 'No, you ring them'. . . 'You ask them', 'No, you ask them. I don't want to ask.'

The downsides of not asking for Yes are heavy. Excellent ideas do not get to fruition. They are left lying on the shelf or in somebody's file. Someone else uses our idea later because we did not ask for the yes.

We may have prepared the ground, planted the seeds, watered the plants and then never harvested the fruits of our labour. Another person comes along, resurrects the idea and, knowing how to ask for Yes, does so and gets our results.

We waste time if we go through the process of preparing our opening, preparing our cogent arguments, knowing which objections may arise and knowing how to handle them if we do not have the courage, if that is what it takes, to ask for the Yes.

And of course we all learn from our experiences. If we forget to ask and do not get the results we want, we inadvertently teach ourselves not to ask next time.

I find that salespeople I meet at my courses often have not sold as much as they might. This is not because they do not know how to sell, far from it. They simply do not use the skills they have as much as they could. Often the skill that is used the least is 'asking for Yes'.

How are we going to make sure that we ask for Yes on every possible occasion?

Asking is easy if:

- We know the words to use.
- We practise those words and phrases.
- We create a habit of asking.
- We ask, easy to ask and easy to answer, questions.
- We only ask when we have belief in what we are saying.

The only way to learn *when* to ask is to risk asking too soon and too often. We will never find out when to ask by asking too late and too infrequently.

## Asking for Yes

What I will do now is share with you a numbers of ways in which you can ask for an agreement, can ask for that Yes. You will need to create the habit and practise the ideas.

### 1. The 'If' Question

First we need to create a new habit. This is to avoid a simple 'Yes' when you will get a better result by responding with an 'If' question instead. Let me explain:

You are in a meeting and people keep asking questions about your idea or proposal.

'Will this work with only two people?' might be a question you are asked.

If you know that the idea WILL work with two people, it would be easy for you to answer 'Yes'. However, that will not lead anywhere. I am suggesting to you that you use 'If' instead, as follows:

'Would your idea work with just two people?'

You respond: 'Would you like it to work with just two people?'

Probable answer: 'Yes.'

You continue: '*If* it would work with just two people, would you try the idea out?'

By saying 'Yes' to your conditional question which began with 'If', the other person will now also say 'Yes.'

*Examples:*

You are talking to a customer about a product. The customer asks: 'Do you do this in green?' Knowing that you do it in green you do NOT say 'Yes', you ask: 'Would you like it in green?' The customer will usually respond 'Yes.' You then ask: '*If* I can get you one in green, will you order it?'

The children come to you after dinner and ask: 'Please may we have sweets?'

You respond: 'Would you like sweets?' This will guarantee a Yes answer!

'*If* you do the washing up you can have sweets. Will you do the washing up?'

You want a raise in pay. You go to your manager or boss and ask:

'What do I have to do to be paid £5,000 a year more?'

The boss answers with a list of targets to be met or tasks to be undertaken.

You continue: 'So, *if* I . . . (and you repeat the list if you are in agreement with it), you will pay me £5,000 per year more?'

What else can the boss say but 'Yes.' He or she has set the rules. You have only batted the question back, starting with the word 'If.'

A delegate on one of my seminars received a promotion from sales manager to sales director using this idea. He asked the managing director what he had to do to be made sales director. He then followed with the 'If' question and added a time frame for accomplishing the tasks set and the promotion that was to follow.

In order to create the habit of not saying 'Yes' when 'If' would produce the desired result, we need to have fun with the idea until it becomes an ingrained response. Try it at home. When someone in the family asks you to make a cup of coffee, instead of saying Yes, say 'Would *you* like a cup of coffee?' They will always answer 'Yes.' You could the follow it with '*If* I make a cup of coffee, will you . . .' and you can add whatever you like as your condition for making the coffee.

## 2. The Straight Question

The next way we can get an agreement is simply to ask for it. Practise the lines: 'Shall we go ahead then?', 'Is that agreed?', 'What date shall we start?', 'When do we raise the invoice?' and as many other ways as you can think of for asking a direct closing question. By practising the words you will use, you will become comfortable with their use.

## 3. The Alternative Question

With this idea we simply assume that we will receive an agreement or a Yes answer and we suggest two alternatives for the way forward.

*Examples:*
'Would you like the red one or the blue one?'
'Shall we move Tom or Mary?'
'Shall we go for three days or two days?'
'Will you tidy the yard on Monday or Tuesday?'
'Do you want to go to Casa Bianca or the Greek restaurant?'
'Shall we start the idea next week or the week after next?'
There are countless situations in which the alternative question could be used.

## 4. The 'Enough' Question

The word 'enough' can be extremely effective in getting a Yes.
  For example:

> ● 'Do you think that next Monday will be soon enough to start?'

A Yes answer to this question means that we will start on Monday next.
  A No answer to this question means that we will still start, but we need to start before Monday next.

> ● 'Do you think that ten computers will be enough?'

The Yes answer means that ten computers will answer our needs.
  The No answer means that the person wants more than ten!
This is one of the simplest ways of asking for Yes. It takes only a little practice to master its use.

## 5. The Minor Question

If we ask for agreement to a minor part of our idea, the agreement we receive also applies to the major part.
For example:

> • 'Do you think that with the new computer system we should have a second printer?' Anyone agreeing to the second printer must have already agreed in principle to have the new computer.

## 6. The Temperature Question

The temperature question is a technique and as such should be used sparingly. It works as follows:

> • 'On a temperature scale of 1–10, 10 being at the top of the scale, how hot are you now about going ahead with this idea?'

Possible answer: 'About 6.'
'What do I have to do to move you from 6 to 10?'
Followed by: 'So if I . . . (whatever was involved in the answer to the previous question) you will go ahead?'

## 7. Safety in Numbers?

We need a method to deal with those people who will agree to your idea only if they know that others have already agreed. There is a certain percentage of the population who will buy products only once they have been on the market for some time, those products having been tried and tested by others who are still happy with them.
There are two ways to deal with this type of person:

### (a) Feel, Felt, Found

When someone is expressing doubt about going ahead you could say:

    To a kinaesthetic person:   'I understand how you *feel*, I
       had another customer/friend who *felt* the same way and
       what they *found* was . . .' You then go on to explain the
       success that the other person had with your idea.

    To a visual person:   'I *see* what you mean, I had another
       customer/friend who *looked* at it in the same way and
       what they *saw* was . . .'

    To an auditory person:   'I *hear* what you say, I had
       another customer/friend who *said* the same thing and
       what they *told* me was . . .'

You may be able to set up an arrangement whereby the person
who is concerned about going ahead is able to contact someone
who has already expressed satisfaction about having taken the
same path.

### (b) Tin Cupping

Another way of dealing with a person who is doubtful about
your proposals is called tin cupping. This involves obtaining the
names of others who will put their names in your tin cup. In
other words, they will support your idea. This might be before a
presentation to the board, in which case you might get the
other managers to support your new idea.

    In a customer contact you would ask your current happy
customers to put their supportive comments in writing so that
you could show them to potential customers. These are called
testimonial letters and are very powerful tools of influence.

### 8. The 'Do or Die' Question

There are times when we have conversations with someone
who just will not make a decision. This can waste a great deal of
valuable time. There comes a point when we need to know if he
or she will go ahead or if it is a lost cause. This is when we must
use a hard approach, the 'Do or Die' question.

    These are the words to use:

    'Either this is a good idea and we should go ahead now, or it
isn't a good idea and we should forget it. Which is it?'

Now we know that this is a last-ditch attempt and that we may have blown the whole agreement. Sometimes, however, it is better to know where you stand than to keep going back to this person in the vain hope that he or she may eventually say yes.

So there are a number of words and phrases with which you can ask easily for the agreement, ask for the Yes. As I stated at the start of this chapter, these ideas will be of the greatest use if you practise them and practise them until they become old friends that you can call on in your time of need.

# Epilogue

Throughout this book we have explored vast amounts of information – over 300 ideas, methods and techniques. It would be impossible to take them all in during just one reading. I strongly urge you to read the ideas again and again, personalise them by using them as soon as possible so that they filter into your long-term memory.

Before I end let me ask you some questions:

'Have you ever walked on a tightrope?'

'Have you ever seen a tightrope walker?'

'In which year did Blondin walk across the Niagara Falls?'

## It works, doesn't it?

I said at the start of the book that the difference between humans and eagles, fish or elephants was the ability to communicate each with our own kind in such a manner as to be able to share the most complex of ideas, theories and messages.

I am certain that over the whole of this book I have been able to share with you some fascinating thoughts, some strange ideas and some extremely powerful techniques and methods.

I know from my own experiences and from the feedback from those who have used these thoughts, that your use of them will produce the results you want in all your interactions with the people in your life.

By using what I call:

The secrets of . . . Persuasion

The Secrets of . . . Conversation

The Secrets of . . . Communication.

*Good luck in all you do in life.*

*Peter Thomson*

# How to Maximise your Results

In this book I have shared with you over 300 hundred ideas on how you can improve your communication and conversation.

Now I would like to share with you five main ways in which you can maximise the results you will obtain by using those ideas.

## 1. Repeated Readings

It is said that we remember about 5% of what we hear, 25% of what we see and 90% of what we do. If that is true, each time you read this or any other book you will only take in about 25%. Repeated readings are therefore essential to capture all of the ideas discussed.

## 2. The Mind Plays

When you read an idea that interests you, your mind begins to play with that idea and experiments with possible uses of the ideas and methods discussed. You may continue to read on while this is happening and not take in the information you read. We have all needed to re-read the same paragraph of a novel or newspaper again and again because our minds had wandered off on a journey of their own.

When an idea does spark your imagination I suggest that you stop reading and really let your mind explore the possibilities of that idea.

## 3. A Different Mood

Each time we read we are in a slightly different mood. On one day an idea may seem outrageous. On another day the same idea seems reasonable and on yet another day we realise how we use it. Perhaps something may have happened in your life in between readings. You have changed your job or position. You are now with a different partner. Your children have grown up. All manner of changes may have occurred. Ideas that were not relevant for your situation on your first reading may have become the answer you were looking for to solve a current problem or to maximise an opportunity.

## 4. An Action Plan

I suggest that you prepare an action plan to put into immediate use the ideas that you feel are relevant to your current position. The sooner you use a method or idea the sooner you will make it your own.

Decide on a date by which you will have completed the action. Check on that date that you have completed the action.

If we remember 95% of what we do, the sooner you put the ideas into action the more likely you are to remember them and be able to use them at the moment you need them.

## 5. Teach Someone Else

You will recall that the top level of listening is represented in the ability to teach someone else the information we have heard. If each time you read this book you do so with the mindset that you are doing so in order to learn new ideas that you can teach to someone else, you will retain a greater portion of the information.

These five methods will enable you to achieve the maximum success with the ideas, methods and techniques I have shared with you.

*Good Luck*

# Test and Quiz Answers

Listening Test Answers
1   95 (40 divided by A half = 80, plus 15 = 95).
2   No. If she is his widow, he must be dead.
3   Nine and five is 14!
4   There is no dirt in a hole.
5   The second coat goes on THE first (coat).
6   When they meet they will both be the same distance from London.
7   None of them. In TOTAL darkness nothing can be seen.
8   A 20p and a 10p (since ONE of those coins isn't a 10p).
9   Moses didn't take any animals onto the ark. It was Noah.
10   Mount Everest (even though it hadn't been discovered).
Page 45   Denmark Elephant Grey 4
Page 47   Red
           Rose
           Chair
Page 47   SIX
Page 48   15 people
           5 stops
           Your name
Page 49   Carrot or similar shaped vegetable.

# ACTION PLAN

Please use this page to record details of the actions that YOU have decided to take. Decide on a realistic target date by which you will have completed the action. Catch yourself doing it 'right' by noting in the space provided the date of completion.

| ACTION TO BE TAKEN | Target Date | Completion Date |
|---|---|---|
|  |  |  |
|  |  |  |
|  |  |  |
|  |  |  |
|  |  |  |
|  |  |  |
|  |  |  |
|  |  |  |
|  |  |  |
|  |  |  |

# FREE INFORMATION

If you would like free information on the following topics please indicate by ticking the appropriate boxes.

Please send this page or a photocopy of it to me and in return I will send you a FREE audio tape giving you the following:

1   The best idea I ever developed for maximising business, sales and profit!
2   Details of my open seminars.
3   An amusing attitude story entitled, Once upon a time there were two frogs . . .
4   An idea I used in a direct mail piece that pulled a staggering 41% response!

If you are interested in information in all three areas, In-house seminars, Public or Open seminars and audio programmes, simply tick the ALL 3 AREAS box.

| TOPIC | IN-HOUSE SEMINARS | PUBLIC SEMINAR | AUDIO PROGRAMMES | ALL 3 AREAS |
|---|---|---|---|---|
| Personal Development | ☐ | ☐ | ☐ | ☐ |
| Selling Skills | ☐ | ☐ | ☐ | ☐ |
| Communication Skills | ☐ | ☐ | ☐ | ☐ |
| Entrepreneurial Skills | ☐ | ☐ | ☐ | ☐ |
| Management Skills | ☐ | ☐ | ☐ | ☐ |
| Public Speaking | ☐ | ☐ | ☐ | ☐ |
| Memory Skills | ☐ | ☐ | ☐ | ☐ |
| Mind Mapping | ☐ | ☐ | ☐ | ☐ |
| Marketing Strategies | ☐ | ☐ | ☐ | ☐ |
| Teamwork | ☐ | ☐ | ☐ | ☐ |
| Leadership | ☐ | ☐ | ☐ | ☐ |
| Customer Service | ☐ | ☐ | ☐ | ☐ |

If you would like details of Peter Thomson as a guest
speaker at your conference or seminars please tick this box   ☐

| Name | Position |
|---|---|
| Company | |
| Address | |
| Address | Post Code |
| Telephone No | No. of Staff |

Please return this page or a photocopy of it to:
Peter Thomson   PO Box 666   Warwick   CV34 6YW
Tel 01926 339901   Fax 01926 339139

Now, you can listen and learn how to make the most of your interaction with others...

## Peter Thomson's

# CONVERSATION
## The Power of Persuasion

AUDIO LEARNING PROGRAMME

from Nightingale Conant

ON 30 DAY FREE TRIAL

Conversation - the art of communicating your thoughts and ideas to others - is one of today's most critically important success skills. In business, in your social life, in your school life, you need to have the ability to get your point of view across to others.

Yet Communication Skills are not taught in schools or colleges, nor discussed in business programmes or tutor groups. Until very recently, few people had ever taken the trouble to master it.

Now, in this powerful 6-audio cassette programme, Peter Thomson, Britain's leading Personal Development strategist shares the results of his studies into the extraordinary power of verbal communication and explains how you can learn the secrets of literally talking your way to success.

* *You'll learn the incredible psychological advantage you can exert on others by choosing the words and phrases to use in any conversation.*

* *You'll learn how to establish instant rapport with total strangers*

* *How to turn hostile verbal adversaries into supportive allies with just a few deft phrases*

* *How to 'read' body language and use it to your advantage.*

In **CONVERSATION The Power of Persuasion** you will learn hundreds of tried and tested techniques which you can use in virtually any situation to help you accomplish your goals.

What's more you can take advantage of Nightingale Conant's remarkable **30-DAY FREE TRIAL** offer to try **CONVERSATION The Power of Persuasion**, without risk or commitment.

Simply call FREEFONE 0800 387869 or FAX 01803 557148 for your 30 DAY FREE TRIAL without risk or commitment. If after 30 days you feel the benefits of the programme far outweigh the cost of just £49.95 (inclusive of VAT, post & packing), send your remittance. Otherwise, you may return the programme and you will owe nothing.

## CONVERSATION -
## You'll never be lost for words again!

**Nightingale Conant**    Long Road, Paignton Devon TQ4 7BB    Phone: 01803 666100 Fax: 01803 557148

# In the hurly-burly of modern life, give yourself the critical edge...

## Peter Thomson's
# ACCOMPLISHMENT
### The Science and Practice

**AUDIO LEARNING PROGRAMME**

from **Nightingale Conant**

ON **30 DAY FREE TRIAL**

Born of more than 20 years at the cutting edge of British commerce, **ACCOMPLISHMENT The Science and Practice** is a stunning guide to self-empowerment, giving you the means to take hold of your life and take control of your direction.

In this powerful 6-cassette programme, Peter Thomson takes you through the essential steps to achieve more, explains more than 500 tried, tested and proven methods and techniques, then shows you what actions you should take to make these techniques work for you.

### *You'll learn:*

* *How to smash your self-limiting beliefs*

* *How to tap your potential for creativity, decision-making and MONEY-MAKING!*

* *How to manage time, people - and your own life*

* *How to criticise constructively*

* *How to become more positive, take action and get results*

### *and much, much more...*

**ACCOMPLISHMENT The Science and Practice** is available exclusively from Nightingale Conant and is available on **30-DAY FREE TRIAL** without risk or commitment.

**PLUS FREE BONUS TAPE** Each programme includes a free bonus tape specially recorded by Peter Thomson as a powerful supplement to the main programme to guide you into and out of each day.

Simply call **FREEFONE 0800 387869** or **FAX 01803 557148** to obtain your copy of **ACCOMPLISHMENT The Science and Practice.** Listen... learn... then after 30 days you decide whether the programme benefits outweigh the cost of just £49.95 (inclusive of postage & packing).

**Now you can achieve that feeling of self-congratulation which only comes with true ACCOMPLISHMENT, every day of your life!**

**Nightingale Conant**   Long Road, Paignton Devon TQ4 7BB   Phone: 01803 666100  Fax: 01803 557148